T0072492

From Adam's Mortality
to
Jesus' Immortality

Despoina Tsaousi

From Adam's Mortality
to
Jesus' Immortality

For as in Adam all die,
so also in Christ all will be made alive.
1 Corinthians 15:22

PARTRIDGE
A Penguin Random House Company

To order additional copies of this book, contact
Partridge India
000 800 10062 62
orders.india@partridgepublishing.com

www.partridgepublishing.com/india

CONTENTS

A study dedicated to
Mahayogi Swami Buddh Puri 'Maharaj Ji'.

Whose pure eyes and compassionate heart
became the actual guide
to decipher
the Ultimate Message of Jesus Christ:
"Whoever lives and believes in me will never die.
Do you believe this?"
John 11:26

*"Holy God, Holy Mighty, Holy Immortal, have mercy on us.
Holy God, Holy Mighty, Holy Immortal, have mercy on us.
Holy God, Holy Mighty, Holy Immortal, have mercy on us.
Glory be to the Father, and to the Son, and to the Holy Spirit,
both now and ever and to the ages of ages. Amen."*

'Trisagion', the Thrice Holy Hymn

FOREWORD

It was April of 2011 when the conception of this study took place by the Divine Grace. I was travelling to India in order to join, for one more time, my spiritual family there. I thought of carrying a gift for my spiritual teacher 'Maharaj Ji' but what would a monk need! A book of an elder from the Mount Athos[1] was all that I could think of presenting to him. Since the celebration of orthodox Easter was about to take place, glorifying the Crucifixion and the Resurrection of Jesus Christ, I also picked a greeting card depicting a picture of Jesus after resurrection. However, little did I know this card would become the source of constant discussions, explorations and insightful notes unfolding the essential message of Jesus Christ, which would finally take shape of this very book!

Those days, Maharaj Ji used to come out from his cell every afternoon in order to greet all of us—his spiritual children—and quench the thirst of our spiritual inquiries with penetrating words that emanate from self-realization and deep practice. After saluting him, I placed those offerings in his hands with innermost piety and humility. They were, as always, welcomed with appreciation and loving kindness of a

---

[1]   *Mount Athos is home to 20 Eastern Orthodox monasteries in Northern Greece. It is commonly referred to as the "Holy Mountain". Nowadays over 2,000 monks from Greece and other Eastern Orthodox countries live an ascetic life in Athos.*

true father. Somehow, the picture of Jesus Christ on the card caught his attention.

He was examining it for some time when he finally turned towards me asking: "Which scene of Christ's life is exactly being presented here?" I replied thoughtfully, realizing the depth of his question, "Maharaj Ji, this is a scene after His Resurrection and it shows that with His death He actually managed to win over the death". Maharaj Ji became more interested and called me closer pointing towards the picture: "Do you see these signs of scars at His hands and feet? Do you believe they should be there since the scene is after the Resurrection? I feel something is missing here. Let me check the Bible and we will discuss further about it".

The entire day, I kept on thinking about his comment and wondered what he actually meant. The next day, during a similar gathering, I approached Maharaj Ji for salutation. As I bowed before him, I listened to his words: "I found the exact part at the Gospel of John where Thomas claims that he will not believe that Jesus was resurrected unless he sees and touches the scars of the nails in His hands. Although it is mentioned very lucidly that after the Resurrection, Jesus appeared before His disciples in His immortal body that was very much tangible, still there is no mention that His body carried these signs of Crucifixion. After all, how an immortalized body could carry any sign of damage or decay, which occur due to the very physicality of the body? We need to further explore the exact section in the Holy Bible".

This first dialogue, inspired from this simple Easter card, initiated a whole new route of study of the Old and New Testament in the following years. It led to a series of eye-opening discussions about the deeper meanings of Jesus' teachings. These enlightening discussions lasted for more than 3 years and gradually they revealed the vastness and depth of

Jesus' teachings. The seed of faith in Jesus, which was sown in this heart as a young child being born in an orthodox Christian family but had remained latent, sprouted and started developing quickly. Jesus, the tender Shepherd, was felt so close in the heart like never before and His messages became the most reliable compass in the journey of life. Traveling earnestly the covert lanes of Holy Bible, we explored their length and breadth. This exploration essentially demands to do the work of the Lord as it is perfectly reflected in Apostle Paul's epistle: *1 Corinthians 15:50-53 "Now I say this, brothers, that flesh and blood can't inherit the Kingdom of God; neither does corruption inherit incorruption. Behold, I tell you a mystery. We will not all sleep, but we will all be changed, in a moment, in the twinkling of an eye, at the last trumpet. For the trumpet will sound, and the dead will be raised incorruptible, and we will be changed. For this corruptible must put on incorruption, and this mortal must put on immortality."*

This essence can definitely be experienced by all those sincere aspirants who yearn for nothing else but union with God; who devote each iota of their existence to glorify God, to serve Him in every form of His creation without any reservation and who sincerely seek of *'being children of the resurrection'* as it is stated in Bible: *Luke 20:36 "For they can't die any more, for they are like the angels, and are children of God, being children of the resurrection."* Jesus' message about the revelation of our inherent immortal nature calls out all those who turn their focus inwards, exploring the Kingdom of Heaven that lies within their hearts, and to all those who follow the path of Jesus, to manifest the Holy Spirit even at the lowest levels of physicality. Jesus inspires and guides such aspirants through the holy closing statement of the *Apostles Creed Prayer "I anticipate the resurrection of the dead and the everlasting life. Amen."*

The main purpose of this study is to spread such seeds of inspiration to all those who aspire to unravel and reflect Jesus' flawless wisdom in their daily lives. The path to this is of course through the purification of the mind and transubstantiation of the physical body i.e. transformation of its perishable earthly constituents into their ultimate Christ–like potential. However, there are various obstacles or knots in the body and mind, which prevent it from becoming a living reality. The root of these knots, which actually signifies the original sin, stems from the ignorance of our true nature. Owing to this ignorance, we identify with our physical bodies and acquire a strong sense of individuality, isolating ourselves from the all–pervading God.

The ultimate goal of this study is to strengthen the zeal, devotion, discrimination, and renunciation of such readers, who wish to enliven the spirit of Jesus Christ's message in their own resurrection and consequent immortalization.

The compassionate guidance of Swami Buddh Puri Ji Maharaj who embodies and expresses the spirit of Holy Scriptures speaks through the pages of this book. Special mention is also due to Swami Suryendu Puri Ji Maharaj for being a precious and veracious companion in this study and writing. Let's unfurl our sails and enjoy this journey with clarity of mind and innermost peace.

October 2015, Athens
One of His children
Despoina Tsaousi

AN INTRODUCTION

"From Adam's mortality to Jesus Immortality", this book is actually a depiction of the extraordinary journey from earth to heaven, from mortality to immortality, from man to divine that Jesus made in this physical plane. This unique journey took place in His physical body, in His flesh and blood in order to set an example before the whole humanity about its divine predestination. He was born as a man and he died too like a man. Not just to leave His body behind as a mortal being. But to come back, through His Resurrection, in His immortalized body and prove that death is not the final destiny. He accomplishes the victory upon death with His death. He proves with His perfect example before our eyes that the only common destiny we all share is the eternal life and the absolute union with God.

Time has come to remove the cataract of our eyes caused by our ignorance and face the truth incarnated in Jesus Christ. Time has come to unfold the following pages...

Jesus Christ the Theanthropos

Jesus Christ is the manifestation of the divine Logos in the earthly world, the God man, the *Theanthropos* as is termed in Greek language and in Him, humans see themselves complete and eternal. He has exhibited throughout His life, simultaneously, the Perfect God and the Perfect Human. With His Resurrection, He triumphs over death; He annihilates "the body of death" as ontological reality; He liberates humankind from mortality. He gives to it the eternal life, the eternal truth, the eternal love, the eternal justice, the eternal Joy and all the other eternal divine goods, which only the God of love and charity is able to offer. He is acknowledged worldwide as the Teacher of compassion, service, unconditional love, humbleness, and forgiveness. Literally, His teachings spread the message of universal brotherhood and build a firm ground for a peaceful and devotional way of thinking and living accordingly.

Aspirants all over the world contemplate upon the spiritual values and moral principles, which are presented in the Bible and each one tries, to his own ability, to follow them and apply in his life. It is true that having Jesus' teachings as a compass throughout life, one can sagely face the waves of adversities and spiritual obstacles, and feel content and happy by loving and serving others.

Still the core of His words seems to be focused in higher realms of actual Christian hood than merely adopting the appropriate Christian behavior. Approaching the Bible with an open mind and a faithful heart, a reader will certainly notice in several verses of the Old, and especially of the New Testament, the calling of Jesus for the *eternal life*. The gist of His teachings vibrates clearly in the following verses: *1 John 2:15-17 "Don't love the world, neither the things that are in the world. If anyone loves the world, the Father's love isn't in him. For all that is in the world, the lust of the flesh, the lust of the eyes, and the pride of life, isn't the Father's, but is the world's. The world is passing away with its lusts, but he who does God's will remains forever."*

What could be the actual meaning of His statement "*he who does God's will remains forever*"? It is an inevitable question, bound to arise in any serious reader of the Holy Bible since it is stated at various places in the biblical canon. The above verse points towards two paths that a being can choose: The first and the more common one is to go after the world and its objects. Since the world is perishable, the traveler of this path is also bound to perish. The other path is the one towards God Himself. Those who travel this path live forever. But the doors of this second path open only through the key of unswerving faith and sincere longing, like that of the fish for water. This is truly indicative of the unceasing call of Jesus for attaining, through union with God, *eternal life or immortality* and for crossing any limitation, any bondage through this union. As it is written at the Gospel of *Luke 18:27 "And he said, 'The things which are impossible with men are possible with God.'"*

The Eternal Life

The grandeur of Jesus' message upon immortality and eternal life is revealed to those who crave to dive and merge deeply into it; to those who strive to reflect its vastness and truth in them by being His innermost disciples, following His example literally by believing and pursuing the eternal life, which Jesus is offering: *1 John 2:24-25 "Therefore, as for you, let that remain in you which you heard from the beginning. If that which you heard from the beginning remains in you, you also will remain in the Son, and in the Father. This is the promise which he promised us, the eternal life."* The eternal life is the predestination of every human and it is reached through the twin steps of resurrection and consequent immortalization in both spirit and flesh. Spiritual practice combined with feverish service becomes the means for this metamorphosis, for this divine revelation and fusion with the Lord: *Philippians 3:20-21 "For our citizenship is in the heavens, whence also a Savior we await – the Lord Jesus Christ – who shall transform the body of our humiliation to its becoming conformed to the body of his glory, according to the working of his power, even to subject to himself the all things."*

Jesus has paved a concrete path before us and calls us to explore its magnitude till the end where life awaits us free from death. Characteristically and candidly Jesus speaks about the means to eternal life throughout Bible using various allegorical terms as those of *water of life — John 4:13-14 "Jesus answered her, 'Everyone who drinks of this water will thirst again, but whoever drinks of the water that I will give him will never thirst again; but the water that I will give him will become in him a well of water springing up to eternal life.'" and bread of life — John 6:47-51 "Most certainly, I tell you, he who believes in me has eternal life. I am the bread of life. Your fathers ate the manna in the wilderness, and they died. This is the bread which comes down out of heaven, that anyone may eat of it and not die. I am the living bread which came down out of heaven. If anyone eats of this bread, he will live forever. Yes, the bread which I will give for the life of the world is my flesh."*

What may Jesus really mean by using the terms *water of life* and *bread of life*? What could He actually mean by announcing that His flesh will be the bread of everlasting life for all those who will eat it? Seeking answer to these and similar questions would lift the mist from these allegories. It would help us understand and explore the meaning of what we have already been hearing from the scripture yet we could not completely relate to it. We could further contemplate why we fall prey to the cruel hands of our ultimate enemy—death, and remain deprived of our citizenship in heaven despite having Jesus, the immortal, on our side.

Death - The last enemy

Jesus defeats, with His Resurrection, the last enemy—death. His immortalized body abolishes the darkness of death and spreads the light of divinity to all His mortal children:

Hebrews 2:14-15 "Seeing, then, the children have partaken of flesh and blood, he himself also in like manner did take part of the same, that through death he might destroy him having the power of death – that is, the devil – and might deliver those, whoever, with fear of death, throughout all their life, were subjects of bondage." He becomes the chariot of eternal life for all those who listen to His message and crave, more than anything else, to join Him in the journey of immortality. Each cell of His immortalized body, after the resurrection, transmits the gist of His teachings, for all those who have faith in Him and are willing to be liberated from the limitations and bindings of mortality. The trumpet of resurrection glorifies the victory of Jesus upon the last enemy—death, and invites us to experience it for ourselves by Divine Grace.

Studying carefully the Bible, in order to imbibe the essence of Jesus' teachings for the most crucial moment, the moment of death, we realize that Jesus provides us with the most vigorous virtues/qualifications. Such qualifications will enable us to face this last enemy, consciously and boldly. Jesus Christ, through His teachings, emphasizes upon the significance of *mental purification* from all the ill thoughts, which cause lust, greed, anger, attachment and selfishness in us. This purification is attained through unceasing recitation of God's name and honest prayer. Jesus also emphasizes upon the *expansion of heart and forgiveness* through unconditional service and love towards all beings. He further accentuates sincere renunciation and unswerving focus on the Creator Himself. These are the essential means, which will prepare us to win our last enemy and enjoy the *water and bread of eternal life.*

It is very important to clarify at this point that the last enemy, which is meant to be destroyed, is death itself, *not only the fear of death.* Jesus calls His disciples to dive into the ocean of eternal life and experience for themselves the grandeur and perfection of the divine kingdom through each cell of their physical bodies. He doesn't merely ask His devotees to be courageous at the moment of death, but to win this barrier literally, to root out the actual source of all sufferings, which is to confine our divine nature in the limits of this perishable mortal body. This limitation disconnects us from God and forces us to believe that "I am just this physical body". Adapted to this belief, we relate with the world and worldly pleasures forgetting that we essentially belong to the heavenly Father and inherit His divine qualities.

Reading the following part of Paul's Epistle to the Corinthians, we can clearly understand that those who belong to Christ and own the precious virtues of spiritual brotherhood, of expansive love and service, of humility and unselfishness, have the essential means to walk to the ultimate destination, to merge into the Divine and be transformed at every level, let that be spiritual, mental, intellectual and even physical. These virtues are but the milestones to keep us on the eternal and eventually lead us to the expansive land of God, which is the goal. Paul writes: *1 Corinthians 15:21-26 "For since death came by man, the resurrection of the dead also came by man. For as in Adam all die, so also in Christ all will be made alive. But each in his own order: Christ the first fruits, then those who are Christ's, at his coming. Then the end comes, when he will deliver up the Kingdom to God, even the Father; when he will have abolished all rule and all authority and power. For he must reign until he has put all his enemies under his feet. The last enemy that will be abolished is death."*

Naturally, we wonder about the meaning of Apostle Paul's words "*for as in Adam all die, so also in Christ all will be made alive.*" In Adam, in the mortal state, dominate the passions, the delusion, the ignorance and the physical limitations. In Christ, all these cease to exist and give their place to peace, awareness, eternal bliss and freedom from any type of dependence or limitation. The ultimate purpose of our life is to rejoin these two states, of Adam and Christ. Now we are living in Adam, at the mortal state. Once we will be united to Christ's consciousness, we will live in Christ and attain immortality. As we know any form of union between two kinds presupposes the existence of life, of consciousness and having common properties e.g. water merges into water and fire into fire. Human is the most conscious being in this world and he has been made according to God's image, thus he holds all His qualities within him in seed form. So, undoubtedly he is qualified by his nature for this union. Nevertheless he has to explore himself the way to achieve this union. The Bible will help us to understand how to bridge this gap between Adam and Christ, between mortality and immortality. It will guide us perfectly so that we will be able to reestablish our life in Christ and reside in our eternal abode, the kingdom of heaven that lies within us.

Bible: The Lighthouse of Wisdom

How will all those who belong to Christ be made alive? How will they all tread the path that leads to the spring of *the water of eternal life,* to the path of *immortality* and *divine transformation?*

The Bible itself is the most reliable guide to answer these questions and direct the true aspirants, who seek nothing but truth, to decipher the actual message of Jesus. Having the wisdom of Jesus as a compass, based on the writings of His disciples in the New Testament, and the testimonials of Old Testament as a lighthouse, we shall explore the various layers of Jesus' teachings in the Bible. Certainly the Bible is written with allegorical terms but not to confuse an aspirant rather enthuse him to search their actual meaning and apply it in their day to day life. Undoubtedly, the study of Bible becomes a living process, brimful of inspirations, for the sincere readers who are ready to reflect these teachings in their body, mind and spirit. This results in regular and pious practice and sharpens their discriminating ability. This power of discrimination will qualify them to understand more subtle meanings in Jesus' teachings and eventually uplift their consciousness to the supreme heights, to that of Christ's consciousness. Following the traces of the holy feet of Jesus and walking with steadfast determination on the path of eternal life that Jesus paved with His Resurrection, they will approach gradually Bible's meanings with further clarity and maturity. Deep the practice is, deeper this understanding will be. The same verses of Bible, each single day as the petals of a lotus, will flourish and will reveal constantly their outstanding beauty and essence before the eyes of those sincere practitioners and readers. Moreover, they will have further inspiration and aspiration to sail in the sea of God in the most reliable and safe boat, that of burning and unswerving faith.

Before completing this introduction, let's recall His words to Martha, Lazarus' sister, from the *Gospel of John 11:25-26* "*Jesus said to her, 'I am the resurrection and the life. He who believes in me will still live, even if he dies. Whoever lives and believes in me will never die. Do you believe this?'*" Now the question directly turns to us. Do we believe this? Do we believe it completely and literally or do we select the parts from His teachings, which suit our mental state and don't deprive us of comfort in our worldly life, deprive us yet of the grandeur of His call? Are we really ready to bid farewell to our dry rationalism and superficial understanding of Jesus' teachings and adopt the innocent eyes and the faithful heart of a child? Are we willing to believe, explore and reflect upon Jesus' teachings with such purity, openness and positive approach that only a child can have in its heart? *Luke 18:16-17 "But Jesus called for them and said, 'Let the little children come to me, and do not stop them; for it is to such as these that the kingdom of God belongs. Truly I tell you, whoever does not receive the kingdom of God as a little child will never enter it.'"*

The present study and elaboration of the Bible is addressed to those who are thirsty and who feel, while reading the following verses from the last chapter of the Bible, the burning craving to answer seriously these questions, respond to this call and receive with open heart and mind the water of Life which emanates from the magnanimous source—Jesus Christ.

Revelation 22:17

"And the Spirit and the Bride say, Come;
and he who is hearing – let him say, Come;
and he who is thirsting – let him come;
and he who is willing –
let him take the water of life freely."

GENESIS

The significance of Genesis

Genesis is the first book of the Old Testament and it is considered to be written by Moses. The name *Genesis* emanates from the ancient Greek term *'gignesthai'* that means birth, beginning, origin. The book starts by describing the creation of the universe and the origin of the human race; narrates the beginning of sin and suffering in the world; continues with the history of early ancestors of Israelites, particularly of Abraham; and ends with the promise that God will continue to guide all those who have faith in Him.

Genesis abounds with numerous figurative expressions and its study demands great attention and caution in order to unlock the various hidden connotations. A panoramic view of it is suggestive of the *providence* of God—the Creator, who takes care of every creature and who *resides inside each one of them*; the divine breath that gives life to *human beings* who are essentially *made to be like God*; the meaning and the root cause of the *original sin;* and the affirmation that God will keep on showing *His concern and mercy* to all His creatures.

In the course of our study, it is really important to comprehend the meaning of the original sin of Adam and Eve (who symbolize the whole humankind), which is the chief cause that deprives humans of the eternal life, disconnects them from God and brings about their exile from His divine kingdom (The Garden of Eden).

However, it wouldn't be unwise to first contemplate the initial verses of Genesis related to the creation of the universe to paint an overall backdrop to our study. The Genesis has beautifully described the divine presence inside every single creature and the divine source from which all in the cosmos are originated. Initially the divine consciousness covers everything that exists in a formless state. At this stage the Light of all the lights, the Logos, which constitutes the beginning of this cosmos, has not yet expanded and the creation has not taken place. Before the creation everything is engulfed in total darkness since still there is no light of manifestation of anything and the spirit of God moves over all the elements which exist in a seed form, in their subtlest state, not yet visible: *Genesis 1:2 "[...] and the Spirit of God moved upon the face of the waters."* The spirit of God spreads the life and sets everything in motion, blowing the vital force that emanates the beginning of creation. The commands of God signal the process of creation of the universe and humankind, a process which actually lasts for billions years, presented yet symbolically within the duration of 'seven days'.

The 'seven days' of creation

How many have been the times in our life we admired the bewitching beauty of this universe and wondered: "Who is behind all these?", "How these all have been created?" Humans have tried to give various answers to these fundamental questions from several fields of their research viz. science, philosophy and religion. Nevertheless, we have realized that such elaborations rely on certain presumptions, which in turn are based on their limited observations thus far.

Genesis, the first chapter of Old Testament in Bible, explains through a wonderful code of symbolical terms, the process of creation and calls us to witness it, standing on the side of God and watching the whole process during the 'seven days' of creation. These allegorical 'seven days' correspond to different stages of creation at causal, subtle and gross/physical levels, which last for billions of years before the universe assumes its present form.

At the primordial stage, before the creation, there is nothing but God—the Creator. A state of blissful stillness or nothingness prevails because the Creator exists in and by Himself. There is no sign of any emanation or creation in this state as there is no external activity and no outward motion. The seed of creation appears in form of God's will. This seed being derived from God carries His power and grandeur, and initiates the process of creation. God sets up the platform for creation by forming heavens and earth. Heavens actually represent the middle link between God and earth—the manifestation of His energy and power in gross/physical form. The radiation of His vast sun is so subtle and ethereal that cannot be confined into any physical limit as it is. Thus it is distillated through the intermediate plane/layer of heavens which becomes the celestial 'sky' that connects God to earth, immortality to mortality, subtleness to grossness. Through the formation of heavens God provides the perfect flute from which the eternal sound of His will is flowing and vibrating the palpitation of this universe: *Genesis 1:1-2 "In the beginning God created the heavens and the earth. And the earth was waste and void; and darkness was upon the face of the deep: and the Spirit of God moved upon the face of the waters."* Earth has not taken shape yet and it is empty since the creation is happening at causal level. This conceptualization signals the beginning of creation that would lead to further differentiation from one to many, from absolute inertness to extreme activity, from a silent Creator to a vivid creation. In Genesis, we are granted to witness in utter lucidness the whole process of creation—how divine wish unfolds and manifests this multilayer and multiform cosmos.

The creation is still in the womb of *the waters,* the divine source, and it is clouded by the *darkness* of the unrevealed state. A spark of light is needed to remove these clouds that veil the rays of the creation, which is about to initiate, as it is described in the following verse: *Genesis 1:3 "Then God said:'Let there be light'; and there was light."* This very command of God sets out the process of creation by establishing the ground for the further formation of the triptych: time, space and causality: *Genesis 1:4-5 "And God saw the light, that it was good: and God divided the light from the darkness. And God called the light Day, and the darkness he called Night. And there was evening and there was morning, one day."* The light of manifestation signals the passage from formless state to formation, from inertia to action and results in emanation of this universe. This alternating occurrence of day and night essentially indicates the eternal cycle of evolution and involution under the provision and shelter of God. The primordial ground of absolute darkness and silence gives way to light and the Logos. The tremendously powerful will of God is actually the Logos, the primordial sound of creation: *John 1:1-5 "In the beginning was the Word, and the Word was with God, and the Word was God. The same was in the beginning with God. All things were made through him. Without him was not anything made that has been made. In him was life, and the life was the light of men. The light shines in the darkness, and the darkness hasn't overcome it."*

During the first day, conception of creation takes place at causal level and gradually passes from the subtle to the gross level and becomes a physical reality. To understand deeper this gradational process of creation we can use an analogy of a seed's journey. However, this analogy should be perceived under the light of a very subtle and extensive scope in order to protect us from the possibility of a shallow and limited perception of such a sophisticated process. We all know that the farmer, the seed and the cultivation constitute three fundamental factors for the journey of a seed. These three factors that are individual and different from each other represent the common triptych of causality: a doer, his deed and the result. However, at the celestial ground we need to adopt a pioneering approach since the farmer, the seed and the act of cultivation here constitute just one entity—God. Being omnipresent, omniscient and omnipotent, it's His nature to manifest Himself in myriad of varied forms. He and the seed, the divine will, become synonymous. This seed is extraordinarily intelligent and capable to attract all the necessary provisions and circumstances that are required for its growth and evolution. As water wets, as fire burns similarly the inherent nature of God is expansion, evolution and creation. In Himself, He emanates this whole universe which is nothing else but Him. He is blissful with the concept of the creation, which reflects His supreme compassion for everything that lives, evolves and exists in Him. He further extends this concept on the second day to allow this seed to evolve.

Thus on the second day the "*water*" and the "*sky*" are formed at a subtle level: *Genesis 1:6-7 "God said, 'Let there be an expanse in the middle of the waters, and let it divide the waters from the waters.' God made the expanse, and divided the waters which were under the expanse from the waters which were above the expanse; and it was so."* From the divine *waters* or the source, the water needed to commence this current of life at lower levels, is separated. This water will ooze the life in the seed and spread its living force in it for its survival and growth. Sky is also formed to provide room for the growth and expansion of the seed. The providence of God for His creation is so vast that He takes care of all the parameters that will be required for the development of the seed of life.

So we move on to the third day of creation, realizing through this beautiful chapter of Genesis the grandeur and wisdom of the Creator who sets the platform for creation, divides it in categories, and assigns specific attributes to each one of them. Everything carries His divine presence being an inseparable part of Him, since everything emanates from Him and rests in Him: *Genesis 1:9-10 "And God said, 'Let the waters under the heavens be gathered together unto one place, and let the dry land appear'; and it was so. And God called the dry land Earth; and the gathering together of the waters he called Seas; and God saw that it was good."* Now the earth and the sea have been formed, still in their subtle level, and thus the ground for the living creatures has been established. Due to the presence of earth, plantation can take place and God commands the production of all kind of seeds which are still in their subtle form: *Genesis 1:11 "God said, 'Let the earth yield grass, herbs yielding seed, and fruit trees bearing fruit after their kind, with its seed in it, on the earth'; and it was so."* As we can see lucidly through Genesis, God creates, with absolute perfection and balance, the necessary ground for the evolution of beings.

Initially, at the causal level, His will to create, to manifest Himself in varied forms is expressed. This expression or command is the Logos. This is the magnificent power of Logos—the primordial sound reflecting the palpitation of this universe—that the command, the action and the result appear at once independent from time, space and causality. He and His will are like sea and its waves, so, they are essentially one—omnipresent, omniscient and omnipotent. His will to manifest in different individual forms is actually His nature and this constitutes the seed of life. This seed carries all the divine attributes within it to conduct the process of creation independently. Its divine intelligence sets the appropriate seed–bed, at the subtle level, for its growth and assumes innumerable forms to reveal its grandeur in the form of this universe. Following the crescendo of this evolutionary process, we explore the journey of this seed from the causal to the subtle level and further up to its manifestation at the gross level. At this point we are ready to enter to the fourth day of creation, flowing with the beautiful narration of Genesis that shows how intelligent and genius is the One who has conceived such a perfect concept.

On the fourth day of creation, God commands: *Genesis 1:14-15 "God said, 'Let there be lights in the expanse of sky to divide the day from the night; and let them be for signs, and for seasons, and for days and years; and let them be for lights in the expanse of sky to give light on the earth'; and it was so."* At this stage God sketches, with unparallel dexterity, the magnificent master plan of this universe. Obviously, other than Him, who else could be behind such perfection. To this irreproachable sketch He comes now to pour the indelible colors of creation painting the sun, the moon, the stars. The solar system, with its splendid colors, adds further beauty to this wonderful divine design. At His canvas one may find myriads of golden sunrays, silver hues of moonlight, innumerable quite white droplets of stars. To complete this masterpiece of art, the painting of creation, God blows the harmonious melody that keeps all these light objects in absolute balance. There is a pulling force that keeps them attracted, since they emanate from one source; still they coexist so harmoniously providing for each other, the necessary space. Only He, a divine maestro, could have composed such a perfect universal symphony that is being played since eternity and pleases all with its celestial melody. Accordingly how peacefully day and night coexist, succeeding each other so smoothly and rhythmically. They are divided in two parts still they constitute one entity. Thus the light of the sun, moon and stars ruling over the day and night correspondingly reaches to the earth and signals the origin of seasons, days and years. Through the alternation of seasons, God designs all the testing conditions for the evolution of the seed. Additionally the light objects which are formed will provide all the necessary circumstances for its growth.

How splendid is the process of divine creation! From the initial formless stage of absolute inertia and stillness, this evolutionary process has emanated. This process is revealed slowly and expansively, following a spiral motion. Nothing in this universe remains same, at macrocosmic and microcosmic levels, but moves and changes unceasingly. Change is the only constant characteristic in the path of evolution as we can see in this incessant alternation and harmonious coexistence of day and night that perfectly reflects the spiral motion of creation Similarly, man and woman in this universe are divided, separated yet they complement each other. They constitute a complete entity and their union actually is the cause of the unceasing expansion of this universe as we will see later on in Genesis with Adam and Eve, who are the mould of the humankind.The evolution of this universe, following this spiral motion, expands in every cycle to higher and wider levels. However, despite this continuous expansion, it has an outstanding discipline and regularity. This combination of incessant motion and perfect discipline is a clear evidence of the compassionate supervision of God. In the fourth day of creation God completes the sketch of the seeding–bed, tests all the parameters and circumstances for the cultivation of the seed and now proceeds further to the design of its categories in various forms.

Reaching the fifth day of creation, the first subtle appearance of all the kinds of creation, that live in the water and fly in the air, is fulfilled: *Genesis 1:20 "And God said, 'Let the waters swarm with swarms of living creatures, and let birds fly above the earth in the open firmament of heaven.'"* At this stage of the evolutionary process, water and air, by the divine grace, acquire the ability to sustain life in form of various creatures that can develop within them. Since the necessary ground for their survival is ready and complete, these living beings can assume life; however, they are yet to be materialized at the physical level. The design of creatures in the water and in the air precedes and prepares the ground for the creatures on the land. In absolute harmony with the holy and eternal wisdom of Bible, scientific researches correspondingly prove with evidences, the beginning of living beings' formation in the water, which gradually shifted and evolved on the shore. The multicolored variety of so many different kinds of seeds is indicative of the grandeur of the creator who designs, as a perfect artist, the beauty of this multiplicity in the universe.

Finally, on the sixth day of creation, since the water and air have been qualified to provide the platform for the growth of the beings that will live in them, earth is equally able to extend its hospitality for the development of all kinds of life that will live over or under it. Thus, the formation of all these kinds at subtle level takes place: *Genesis 1:24 "God said, 'Let the earth produce living creatures after their kind, livestock, creeping things, and animals of the earth after their kind'; and it was so."* This crescendo of the wonderful music of the creation becomes complete with the design of the most composite and artful mold, that of the human being, which is granted to reflect perfectly God's image: *Genesis 1:26-27 "And God said, 'Let us make man to our image and likeness: and let him have dominion over the fishes of the sea, and the fowls of the air, and* the beasts, and the whole earth, and every creeping creature that moves upon the earth.' And God created man to his own image: to the image of God he created him: male and female he created them." It is very significant to clarify at this point that the human being is created essentially in God's image. Therefore, humans inherit all the divine qualities and dominion over all the other creatures. As a king, ruling over his kingdom, is more responsible than any other person for the prosperity, safety and development of his kingdom, similarly human beings, male and female, have the power over all the other creatures and carry the highest responsibility to support them. The fact that humans have dominion over all other beings does not entail that they can take advantage of their state or that they are superior to other creatures and have more authority. Because of their advanced intellectual ability, their duty is to assist all the rest beings to grow and protect them from any situation that would hinder their growth. Genesis expresses so lucidly the eternal truth of all the Saints *"We are an integrated and inseparable part of God and hence divinity is our true nature"*.

Eventually the design of every creature at subtle level is completed and as a machine, having been perfectly designed, needs the fuel to be set in motion, similarly it is necessary for the beings to receive an appropriate source of energy and begin the route of their evolution. Hence, God provides for every creature, which has the breath of life in it, the seed-bearing plants as their nutrition: *Genesis 1:29-30 "God said, 'Behold, I have given you every herb yielding seed, which is on the surface of all the earth, and every tree, which bears fruit yielding seed. It will be your food. To every animal of the earth, and to every bird of the sky, and to everything that creeps on the earth, in which there is life, I have given every green herb for food'; and it was so."* At this point being pleased with the platform that He has established for the process of creation, He moves further for its materialization.

At this juncture, it would be wise to consider that the state of humankind, which is being described in this particular verse of Genesis, is before the original sin of Adam and Eve; before their disobedience and succeeding fall. At this state, there is absolute connection with the divine source and the appearance of individualism, selfishness and arrogance has not taken place. On the contrary, the present state of humankind hardly resembles the image of God. The grossness that dominates the body, the outward focus of senses/mind and the strong belief that "I am the doer, I can control everything" cause disconnection from the Creator—God and it certainly does not draw the picture of God.

Therefore, it would not be real and correct to claim that the present state of human beings resembles God, since this state is so filthy and muddy to allow the crystal clear light of God to be reflected in it. However, despite of these cloudy layers, the everlasting sun of God's providence is totally bright. Hence every human being is granted with the manifestation of God through Jesus Christ who becomes the most reliable and flawless link for the reconnection, for the reunion with the divine source. The image of resurrected Jesus matches absolutely in God's image. The lack of grossness at each cell of His immortalized body, the divine stream of unconditional love and compassion towards all the creatures, the absolute obedience to God's will and command without any trace of personal will, all these delineate with ultimate perfection, the image of God. They reassure us about the truth of our divine nature and the necessity of our purification to reach earnestly to our state before the fall, the necessity to respond to Jesus' call in order to regain our true identity, to dive into the sea of eternal life, to merge in the divine.

On the seventh day God rests inside His own creation delighted and pleased since everything has been designed perfectly. There is an expansion of supreme bliss and each and every thing in the universe is qualified now to manifest this bliss and spread the splendid fragrance of His will: *Genesis 2:2 "And on the seventh day God ended his work which he had made: and he rested on the seventh day from all his work which he had done."* At this stage, since the concept and the design of the seed and the seed-bed have been completed, seed of divine will is sown in the earth of divine bliss and it is ready to sprout. The seed has been actuated, the ground has been prepared, and all the necessary factors for its growth have been created. At this stage of the seventh day the process of materialization begins and all the above creatures manifest eventually at the gross/physical level. This materialization signals the beginning of this world in the gross form that we all perceive.

Everything which has been formed and materialized receives now the blessing of God, which is actually the life force: *Genesis 2:3 "God blessed the seventh day, and made it holy, because he rested in it from all his work which he had created and made."* God conveys, through His bliss and grace, the energy, the fuel, the power of life and spreads in everything the rays of His divine nature. Everything carries His properties and has received the blowing of His life giving energy inside it. Thus everything is actually Him, everything is divine. Exploring through Genesis the vastness of this evolutionary process, we realize that He is essentially present in every single thing of this universe. Inside this vast ocean of divine creation, every subjective opinion for the value of something based on our likes – dislikes melts and an expansive respect even for the tiniest particle of this cosmos arises, since in this evolution all is Him and just Him.

Evolution always follows a spiral motion, never a directly straight line. Accordingly, the seed is sown and the energy has been transmitted to it by the divine source. To evolve, to grow, to transform into a beautiful plant now it needs to dissolve inside the earth, break every confinement and go beyond any limitation. First, it has to dissolve completely and then it is able to take a new form and develop into a full-fledged tree. The seed transforms its basic nature and reveals the tree that is existing in it, in a potential form. This tree, standing as a perfect example of the supreme power that is dormant in seed's form, can be an everlasting source of further new seeds and empower them to grow and manifest their latent potential. The predestination of the seed is its development into a tree. Similarly, the evolution of humankind follows the same process. The predestination of human is the divinization and the eternal life in complete union with God. We carry inside us all the divine properties, though in latent form, and through our evolution these properties are meant to spring up and grow. Jesus Christ is the perfect example of our predestination and His life becomes the ultimate source of inspiration and aspiration to unfold the inherent divinity that lies within us. Through His Resurrection, He paves the path for us all and strengthens us to walk on the path with zeal, dignity and burning craving.

Potentially and essentially, we are one with the Creator and our life is a unique chance to unfold and reflect this truth, at mental, spiritual and even physical level. Yet as the seed has to be dissolved, shatter all the limitations and then sprout in order to fulfill its predestination, similarly human has to break all the confinements of the physicality in order to transform his nature, be resurrected and live eternally. Jesus' teachings become the most appropriate seed-bed for the development of the seed of immortality which lies inside us, still in latent form though: *1 Corinthians, 15:36-38 "You foolish one, that which you yourself sow is not made alive unless it dies. That which you sow, you don't sow the body that will be, but a bare grain, maybe of wheat, or of some other kind. But God gives it a body even as it pleased him, and to each seed a body of its own."* Physicality with all its confinements and limitations is the seed that has to die. Then the actual body of human, the resurrected and immortal one, will manifest since this is what God has determined for the humankind. Jesus, the incarnated God, takes flesh and blood, a physical body, and He dissolves it as a seed to reveal, through His Resurrection, the actual predestination of the humankind, which is immortality. He sets an example before our eyes through His life on this earth and with His teachings He makes it available and approachable for every sincere seeker of truth. So vast is the compassion and the grandeur of the Lord!

The tree of life and the tree of knowledge

With the life-giving breath of God, the human being becomes a physical reality and begins to live in the Garden of Eden, which actually represents the heaven on earth: *Genesis 2:7-8 "Then the Lord God formed man from the dust of the ground, and breathed into his nostrils the breath of life; and man became a living soul. And the Lord God planted a garden eastward, in Eden, and there he put the man whom he had formed."* At this level of creation, the visible and gross form of humankind is shaped. It is covered with layers of grossness, yet still it is linked to the higher realms of the divine. The vital force which keeps the human being alive is this divine gust of air, the divine power. When this force leaves the body, the gross form decays and finally disintegrates.

As we have already told Adam, the first human, having obtained a gross/physical form, resides in the Garden of Eden: *Genesis 2:9 "Out of the ground the Lord God made every tree to grow that is pleasant to the sight, and good for food; the tree of life also in the middle of the garden, and the tree of the knowledge of good and evil."* At this point, God gives a direct command to Adam, which lucidly reflects His overflowing compassion and providence towards His creatures: *Genesis 2:16-17 "And the Lord God commanded the man, saying, 'Of every tree of the garden you may freely eat; but of the tree of the knowledge of good and evil, you shall not eat of it; for in the day that you eat of it you will surely die.'"* It is very important at this point to contemplate upon the meaning of these two trees and the particular command that is given to Adam, before we continue with the formation of Eve and the human disobedience to God's request.

Amongst all the trees that exist in the Garden of Eden, one tree gives life and Adam is allowed to eat all the fruits of that tree as of any other tree, except for the tree of knowledge. The tree of life signifies the source of essential and eternal life with which we are continuously connected. This connection can be maintained as long as we remain united with God and recognize our self as an inseparable part of Him; as long as we surrender our ego to the divine's will and rest with innocence, with purity of heart and mind and with childlike love within the lap of divine mother. Unquestionable faith and wholeheartedly devotion qualify us to tread the path with discipline to God's command and ultimately drink the nectar of eternal life. The true eternal life and all its unceasing fruits exist in the connection with God, while the disconnection from Him actually signifies death. Adam is free to eat as many fruits as he wishes from the tree of life which constantly and endlessly produces life-giving fruits and grants him with the eternal life. However, despite of the vast generosity of magnanimous God who provides everyone with the same opportunities; those who have complete faith to the divine are able to taste the ambrosia of His kingdom; those who follow His command and act accordingly, they remain connected unceasingly with Him and enjoy eternal divine bliss. In this state there is no sense of possessing or controlling and the human being infused in the divine consciousness experiences in his totality the expansion of innermost peace, unity and bliss.

The other tree gives the knowledge of good and bad. It is the tree of knowledge of duality. It spreads the sense of judgment, the distinction between good and evil, the sense of dividing. Adam is asked to avoid these forbidden fruits which will turn his focus outwards, which will deprive him from seeing the unity in everything that surrounds him. The knowledge of good and evil will restrict his subtle vision to see God in everything and his eyes will be covered by the grossness and captured in the clouds of duality. One who plucks the fruits of the tree of knowledge will obtain the sense of individuality, a feeling of being separated from others, will identify himself with his physical body and will try to become the 'doer', the 'controller', the 'possessor' believing that he can supersede the role of God. He will be tempted to think that there is actually no need of God and that he can live on his own, totally independent and separated from Him. He will evaluate what is good and evil according to the dodges of his mind and ignore God's guidance and command. Therefore God commands Adam that he must not eat the fruits of that tree, otherwise he will die or in other words he will lose the essence of life, which is the connection with Him. Detachment from God actually entails death and literally the loss of the *eternal life* about which Jesus unceasingly speaks in His Teachings.

Adam-Eve and the appearance of the serpent

Then the Lord God said: *Genesis 2:18 "The Lord God said, 'It is not good that the man should be alone; I will make him a helper suitable for him.'"* Thereby all the animals and the birds are formed but none of them is a suitable companion to help him so the God makes the man fall into a deep sleep and forms a woman out of his rib: *Genesis 2:23 "The man said, 'This is now bone of my bones, and flesh of my flesh. She will be called 'woman,' because she was taken out of Man.'"* In fact male and female are one entity in two forms which originate from the same source, the divine. Woman constitutes the innermost section of man and she is an inseparable part and parcel of him and vice versa. Male and female, together compose actually the totality. Their union is the way to entirety and completeness. Thus male and female equally indicate the totality through their fusion and unity. None is superior or lower than the other rather they both have a complementary and counterbalancing role between themselves. At this state, before their fall and disobedience, Adam and Eve although they are both naked still they feel no embarrassment, since they are not bodily conscious, their senses are not turned outwards being introverted and focused inside. Thus they feel no shame for being naked since they are not conscious of this nudity and experience no distinction due to the absence of their body consciousness.

The appearance of the serpent brings an end to this introverted focus and causes the turning of their senses outwards. The serpent actually signifies the loss of connection with God, the identification with the physical gross body and the activation of senses outwards that will drag humankind to become slave of sensory enjoyments. The serpent is the cause of the outward focus, of the deterioration of the pure inward connection with the life-force, God Himself. Its usual characteristic is to crawl on the ground, so similarly, its power forces the consciousness of Adam and Eve to be involved with the physical world and hinders its link with the higher consciousness that of God. At the beginning of the dialogue between Eve and serpent, Eve is still obedient to the command of God about not to eat fruit from the tree of knowledge or else she and Adam will lose the eternal life and become mortal. The serpent spreads the veil of ignorance and delusion upon Eve by luring her to taste that fruit, to disobey God's command and gain the knowledge of good and evil: *Genesis 3:4-5 "The serpent said to the woman, 'You won't surely die, for God knows that in the day you eat it, your eyes will be opened, and you will be like God, knowing good and evil.'"*

Actually the serpent symbolizes the power of ignorance which deceives Eve and challenges her to open her eyes outwards, to turn the senses to the external world, to obtain the knowledge of good-evil, which is just a worldly notion since everything is essentially divine. The serpent turns her mind towards likes and dislikes; disconnects her from her true nature—the divine; and causes her to identify with a specific individuality based on body consciousness. Eve, fascinated by the delusive idea of becoming wise and equal to God, is captivated by this call of the serpent and finally gives in to this temptation, tasting the fruit herself and offering it, also, to her husband, Adam: *Genesis 3:7 "The eyes of both of them were opened, and they knew that they were naked. They sewed fig leaves together, and made themselves aprons."*

At this point both of them consider themselves as different individuals, realize their different sex and their nakedness and try to cover themselves with utter embarrassment. As long as the serpent crawls, it is actually a dark power that pulls downwards the consciousness of humankind, ensnaring it to passions, instincts, attachments and deceptive conceptions. Nevertheless, when the serpent erects, which symbolically signifies the uplifting of the consciousness of humankind through unceasing prayer and selfless service, it is transforming its dark power to a divine force which can lead the human being to purification, to enlightenment and ultimately to perfection. This erectness of the serpent reminds us about the beautiful definition of the Greek term for human which is called '*anthropos*', it means 'the one who is looking upwards', who has the craving to evolve, advance and move onwards. The inherent nature and the uniqueness of humankind is this everlasting journey to move upwards and accomplish the unity with the ultimate source, the God.

The original sin

Before continuing with the God's judgment for the human disobedience it is important to elaborate further the role of the serpent and the essence of the original sin, of the human fall of Adam and Eve, which causes the loss of the *eternal life*. As we know, the serpent, by the very nature, slithers and cannot rise above the earth's level. Similarly, the acceptance of its challenge—disconnecting Adam and Eve from their true divine nature—now causes the crawling of their bodies on the ground of sensual enjoyments and sexual pleasures, the creeping of the mind in the land of arrogance and selfishness, the turning of their focus to the world outside. This outwards focus blocks the direct link with the ultimate source – God – and the veils of ignorance, about their true origin and nature, disconnect them from the source. Losing the power of this inherent connection, they become unable to discern the significance of God's existence in their lives, condemning themselves to mortality. As their eyes are captured by the glitter of the world, the senses turn outwards and they lose the conscious connection with the life-source within. The turning of senses outwards signals the depletion of life-force and causes the appearance of lust, greed, anger, attachment and egotism. The inner peace and tranquility of divine connection are replaced by disharmony, misery and restlessness. Adam's and

Eve's illusionary belief that they themselves can become like God, considering Him as something discrete and separated from them and identifying themselves as individual physical bodies rather than an inseparable part of Him, defines the human falling—the original sin of humankind.

The original sin is actually the firm belief of human that he can live on his own and that he does not need God's presence, grace and guidance for his development. Enchained in this strong sense of individuality he turns his back towards God losing in this way the direct contact with His everlasting bliss and flawless wisdom. The moment Adam and Eve commit the actual sin and disconnect from their divine source, they obtain a separate individuality and they are deprived of their unique vision to see God inside everything and everyone. They recognize themselves as physical bodies and then they are actually allowing the power of the serpent to drag their consciousness downwards, to be entangled inside the nets of outwards focus and tendencies, to merge into the grossness of physicality and condemn themselves to the clutches of death. As the inherent inwards focus of the senses is now forced outwards, knots are developed at the orifices or the doors of all the senses, which hinder this linkage with the divine grace within and cause our consciousness to downgrade. Due to this atypical process the inner force gradually diminishes and the dominance of mundane activities further extinguishes this force and strengthens the sense of ego, fear, insecurity and doubt.

The reestablishment to our true nature and the overcoming of this original sin, by reconnecting with the ultimate source-God, constitutes the essential and utmost goal of humankind. Such supreme and meaningful goal can be accomplished through unceasing, steady and devotional spiritual practice and prayer combined with compassionate service towards all the beings. Piercing all the knots and uncovering the veils of ignorance and delusion, purifying all the gross and subtle impurities, ultimately we will be able to root out the original sin and be reunited with God, the wellspring of immense bliss, light and wisdom. By redirecting the focus back to the unlimited source away from the worldly attractions, through sincere and regular prayer and practice, the seeker of this reunion will be qualified to reach the ultimate gate of God's kingdom inside the human body. Every sincere devotee who has burning craving and honesty to be united with Him, he will accomplish the essential goal of his life, as long as he seeks nothing but the truth, unconditionally and wholeheartedly. Crystal-clear are the words of Jesus for those sincere seekers: *Matthew 7:7-8 "Ask, and it will be given you. Seek, and you will find. Knock, and it will be opened for you. For everyone who asks receives. He who seeks finds. To him who knocks it will be opened."*

Exploring through Genesis, the magnificent process of creation, we have realized that in this universe nothing is made, done or chosen at random. On the contrary everything is so well designed and has a definite purpose, under the incessant divine provision and plan. Accordingly, the tree of knowledge is a part of the divine plan for the evolution of humankind towards purification, enlightenment and divinization. Adam and Eve obtain, by the divine grace, the individuality and receive thus the ground for the ultimate manifestation of the latent possibilities within. By knowing the duality of good and evil, they become aware of the limitations, the confinements and hence they are able to get over them, to go beyond them.

Adam and Eve, being the carriers of the divine bliss, by tasting the fruits of the tree of knowledge realize the limitations of dualism and this will lead them to expand gradually their vision and understand the vastness of oneness, of unity with God. The divine seed is disseminated within each creature and it will flourish and fructify when the complete discovery and manifestation of the latent possibilities in them is accomplished. While residing in the Garden of Eden, Adam and Eve experience bliss and peace by the divine grace. Having committed the original sin, unknowingly and unconsciously they become deprived of this bliss and peace. Nevertheless, the grandeur of God's compassion provides all the necessary circumstances to regain this celestial state, yet this time consciously, in total awareness, through their personal effort. Realizing the precious value of their connection with God and reconsidering the essence of their life, they are granted, by the divine, to return to their inherent state before the fall and rejoin with the innermost fountain of happiness and stillness. In the vast ocean of the creation, the divine mercy is blowing unceasingly and they are called to play their own role, to unfurl the sails and begin this beautiful journey of endless evolution themselves.

Human disobedience to God's command

Human disobedience to God's command leads to the pronouncement of His Judgment: *Genesis 3:16-19 "To the woman he said, 'I will greatly multiply your pain in childbirth. In pain you will bear children. Your desire will be for your husband, and he will rule over you.' To Adam he said, 'Because you have listened to your wife's voice, and have eaten of the tree, of which I commanded you, saying, 'You shall not eat of it,' cursed is the ground for your sake. In toil you will eat of it all the days of your life. It will yield thorns and thistles to you; and you will eat the herb of the field. By the sweat of your face will you eat bread until you return to the ground, for out of it you were taken. For you are dust, and to dust you shall return.'"* Since they have tasted the fruit of the tree of knowledge, Adam and Eve have actually deprived themselves of the fruits of the tree of life. From now on they are bound to remain at the earth's level and obtain through their efforts the gross nutrition which will keep them alive but not for ever. Before the fall, they are connected to the life-force and being focused internally they don't have to struggle for their nutrition since everything is provided by God. Receiving the providence of God and trusting everything to Him, they are nourished from the unceasing fruits of the tree of life, from the divine subtle nectar, the ambrosia which is being offered to them and which they are capable of accepting due to their innocence and faith.

After the fall, the disconnection from the tree of life takes place. Devoid of this eternal supply of life force, which is actually the union with the God, they are bound to the earth element, to identification with the physical body and the sense of the 'doer' (*you are dust*) and to mortality (*to dust you shall return*). The birth from now on is a painful process which emanates from the sexual union and it is connected with the lowest orifices of the human body. The distinction between the two different sexes raises the sensual desire, the lust, the greed, the passion and the attachment. As long as the creation is upon God's will, God's grace in form of peace and bliss naturally exists everywhere. The moment they disobey the God's command and obtain the knowledge of good and evil they lose the root of the life force and condemn themselves to mortality and death.

Finally, Adam and Eve are sent out of the Garden of Eden: *Genesis 3:22-23 "Then the Lord God said, 'Behold, the man has become like one of us, knowing good and evil. Now, lest he reach out his hand, and also take of the tree of life, and eat, and live forever.' Therefore the Lord God sent him out from the garden of Eden, to till the ground from which he was taken."* A human being gaining the knowledge of good and evil, being entangled mentally into judgments, likes-dislikes and preferences-repulsions behaves like a God and adopts the role of the one who "controls, possesses and acts". Adam and Eve, by obtaining the knowledge of good and bad, they are able to discriminate as God and by knowing which is the tree of life they can eat its fruits with no consideration about the Creator, whose grace has provided everything. They regard themselves as independent individualities that can live eternally on their own, without the need of God. They want to be like God by competing with Him rather than uniting with Him. Before the fall, they are directly connected with God through their innocent heart and unquestionable faith. Being a part and parcel of Him, they carry no personal will, expectation or desire. After the original sin, they lose this direct connection and this elysian bliss and peace. God offers to Adam and Eve the choice to obey to His command and enjoy the eternal life or disobey His will and bind themselves to the mortal state. They have the free will to decide and they carry the complete responsibility for this choice. Undoubtedly everything is following and surrendering to the divine plan, still it is the action of Adam and Eve to disobey the divine command. At this state of ignorance and delusion the human being is bound to mortality and to body consciousness.

The road that leads to the tree of *immortality*, of *eternal life* and *divine bliss*, of *God Consciousness* is blocked due to the outwards focus of the senses, the grossness of the physical body. Additionally the mental impurities and such ill feelings as lust, greed etc. keep the intellect bound to the earth and prevent it from elevating to higher realms of deeper insight and discrimination. Moreover the lack of innocent childlike faith and complete surrender to the God's will hindrance the journey, however it's our predestination to keep on evolving and reconnect with the ultimate source, God.

Returning consciously to the Garden of Eden

The ultimate compassion and mercy of God brings onto earth the One who unblocks the road, who teaches with extreme clarity and lucidness through His life, the way to return consciously to Eden and reside there enjoying the fruits of the tree of eternal life. The One who incarnates the divine, who comes into existence with blood and flesh to teach the people unceasingly, to inspire them through His divine personality and to ensure through His Resurrection that eternal life is meant for each one who surrenders everything to His father, to the Creator, the divine; for each one who reflects through each cell of his existence the message of unconditional love, compassion and service. Before approaching the vastness of the One, of Jesus Christ, we could have at this point of our study a panoramic view of all those great personalities presented in the Old Testament who prepared the ground for His manifestation on earth. Of all those beings who are granted from God to praise unceasingly His glory and who confirm Jesus' words to Thomas when he was asking for visible signs of Him in order to believe that He was resurrected: *John 20:29 "Jesus said to him, 'Because you have seen me, you have believed. Blessed are those who have not seen, and have believed.'"*

OLD TESTAMENT: PREPARING THE GROUND FOR LORD'S DESCENT

Undoubtedly, the Old Testament abounds with numerous stories of great souls whose devotion and burning faith in God shine through the ages and foreshadow the descent of God through Jesus Christ. Moreover, in Old Testament we are granted to come across numerous verses that exhibit so lucidly the power of unquestionable faith and complete surrender to the divine will. These powerful verses, combustible as woods, are able to melt all the impurities and obstacles that may appear during the spiritual endeavor of the devotees and empower their zeal and determination to evolve further. These holy verses with their oceanic depth and celestial height strengthen the flames of one-pointed dedication to God, thus the fire of devotional love reanimates incessantly.

The lineage of Divine Messengers

Abraham

The lineage of all the descendants of Lord starts with Abraham and it is through him that all the nations will be blessed as it is mentioned at *Genesis 18:17-19 "The Lord said, 'Will I hide from Abraham what I do, since Abraham has surely become a great and mighty nation, and all the nations of the earth will be blessed in him? For I have known him, to the end that he may command his children and his household after him, that they may keep the way of the Lord, to do righteousness and justice; to the end that the Lord may bring on Abraham that which he has spoken of him.'"* Abraham symbolizes the example of unconditional faith to God's will and of absolute surrender to Him. He accepts God's command to sacrifice his only son, Isaac, whom he loves so much. The moment he is ready to fulfill God's command with humble obedience he listens to God's words: *Genesis 22:16-18 "'By myself I have sworn, says the Lord: Because you have done this thing, and have not withheld your son, your only son, that I will bless you greatly, and I will multiply your seed greatly like the stars of the heavens, and like the sand which is on the seashore. Your seed will possess the gate of his enemies. In your seed will all the nations of the earth be blessed, because you have obeyed my voice.'"*

Indeed numerous were His descendants and the pinnacle of this vow is attained with the appearance of Jesus Christ. Abraham's case teaches the significance of unquestioning faith beyond doubts and rationalistic approaches. The annihilation of his personal will points out the importance of complete renunciation for any genuine devotee who walks the path of God realization. With feverish renunciation and complete abolishment of the sense of possession, Abraham is offering at the altar his most beloved son in obedience to God's command. As a loyal instrument in the hands of the divine, he has offered himself totally to God and with this sacrifice he experiences the grandeur of divine grace, which leaves no scope for any doubts and dilemmas. Abraham trusts God with all his heart and accordingly becomes a perfect flute through which the celestial music is played. The flute has to be internally empty so that the sounds can be produced, similarly in the case of a sincere devotee absolute emptiness, through unremitting prayer and service, has to be cultivated for the descent of God. His heart, mind, body has to be empty, free from prejudices, attachments, and impurities so that the divine's presence will manifest within him and it will be reflected throughout his totality in mental, spiritual, intellectual and even physical level.

Moses

Moses is the man whom God chooses to lead the people of Israel from Egypt. Due to his purity he obtains from God the authority to present himself before the king of Egypt and bring the Israelites out of Egypt. Moses, with extreme humility, hesitates to speak before the king of Egypt and the Israelites considering himself a poor speaker. He doubts if he is actually qualified for such an important speech in this crucial mission of leading the Israelites out of Egypt. Then God says to him: *Exodus 4:11-12 "The Lord God said to him, 'Who made man's mouth? Or who makes one mute, or deaf, or seeing, or blind? Isn't it I, the Lord? Now therefore go, and I will be with your mouth, and teach you what you shall speak.'"* After leaving Egypt, the Israelites reach Mount Sinai and Moses is the only devotee who is called to the top of the mountain when God will descend there. All the rest of the people are commanded to stay at a boundary around the mountain to see Him and not to go to the top or near the mountain. This divine command indicates the necessity of having an innocent, pure heart in order to be able to meet and experience the glory of God.

When Moses goes up Mount Sinai a cloud covers it: *Exodus 24:16-18 "The glory of the Lord God settled on Mount Sinai, and the cloud covered it six days. The seventh day he called to Moses out of the midst of the cloud. The appearance of the glory of the Lord God was like devouring fire on the top of the mountain in the eyes of the children of Israel. Moses entered into the midst of the cloud, and went up on the mountain; and Moses was on the mountain forty days and forty nights."* Being completely harmonized with God's will, Moses stays with Him for forty days and nights without eating and drinking anything and receives the words of the divine covenant, the Ten Commandments. Moses is qualified for this direct meeting due to his steadfast devotion and unparalleled faith. He becomes the sanctified channel through which God teaches the community of Israel and imparts to it the Ten Commandments.

By transferring to people of Israel, the divine laws of holiness and justice, Moses mentions the law, which Jesus called the second great commandment hundreds of years later: *Leviticus 19:18 "You shall not take vengeance, nor bear any grudge against the children of your people; but you shall love your neighbor as yourself. I am the Lord."* Despite the unceasing human disobedience, Moses continues to praise the name of the Lord and to tell His people about His greatness. Indicative is his song before he leaves his body at the age of a hundred and twenty: *Deuteronomy 32:1-3 "Give ear, you heavens, and I will speak. Let the earth hear the words of my mouth. My doctrine shall drop as the rain. My speech shall condense as the dew, as the small rain on the tender grass, as the showers on the herb. For I will proclaim the name of the Lord. Ascribe greatness to our God!"*

Elijah and Elisha

Prominent in the Old Testament are the prophets of the Lord, those courageous spokesmen of God who warn the people not to worship idols and not to disobey God. Especially notable is the prophet Elijah, who announces to king Ahab, the beginning of the period of drought: *1 Kings 17:1 "Elijah the Tishbite, who was of the foreigners of Gilead, said to Ahab,*

'As the Lord God, the God of Israel, lives, before whom I stand, there shall not be dew nor rain these years, but according to my word.'" Elijah, due to his unceasing contact with the divine, performs this miraculous action of the beginning of drought. His innermost motivation for this apparently strict decision is his compassionate longing to help all those who have gone astray and bring them back to the source of wisdom and bliss, to God.

In a similar case, Elijah, feeling extreme sympathy for the loss of the son of the widow who takes great care of him, asks the Lord to restore the child to life and receives His answer: *1 Kings 17:22-23 "The Lord listened to the voice of Elijah; and the soul of the child came into him again, and he revived. Elijah took the child, and brought him down out of the room into the house, and delivered him to his mother; and Elijah said, 'Behold, your son lives.'"* Like Jesus Christ, the prophet Elijah is a channel through which the divine will manifests and reveals. Elijah travels for forty days and forty nights to Mount Horeb, where Moses had received the Ten Commandments. He is the only person described in the Bible as returning to Horeb, after Moses and his generation had left Horeb several centuries before. Jesus, Moses and Elisha, the faithful successor of Elijah, spend equally the same number of days in absolute isolation independent from any external provision or support. In the New Testament, during the magnificent transfiguration of Jesus before the eyes of Peter, John and James, the divine company of Jesus, Moses and Elisha reunites. These three holy personalities exhibit within themselves the absolute freedom and divinization in every level, breaking all the limitations and confinements, becoming themselves the channel for the divine descent on earth.

The end of the prophets of Baal signifies the end of the drought. While all the people of Israel are trying to kill Elijah, since he is the only prophet left, the Lord commands him to anoint Elisha to succeed him as a prophet. Elisha shows supreme loyalty to Elijah: *2 Kings 2:4 "Elijah said to him, 'Elisha, please wait here, for the Lord has sent me to Jericho.' He said, 'As Yahweh lives, and as your soul lives, I will not leave you.' So they came to Jericho."* When Elijah is taken up to heaven by a chariot of fire pulled by horses, his power is transferred to Elisha through the cloak that is fallen from him. Now Elisha is able to perform miracles like Elijah, strengthening thus people's faith in God. This supreme compassion for the sufferings of the humankind, which happen due to the ignorance and the disconnection from the divine source, oozes from such holy personalities and the nectar of this compassion flows eternally from their hearts. All these miracles are meant to stimulate the flame of faith within the hearts of those who are ready to believe and transform themselves. The prophets prepare with such piety and devotion the path for the ultimate fountain of compassion, in the form of Jesus Christ whose descent signals the absolute salvation and liberation from sorrow, decay and ultimately death.

Job

In the book of Job in the Old Testament the precious story of Job is presented. He is an extremely good and righteous man who suffers total disaster losing all his children and property and being afflicted with a repulsive disease. His friends try to explain his suffering by traditional religious terms: God, as they assume, always rewards good and punishes evil. But for Job this is a too simplistic approach and he reacts to these calamities. He feels he does not deserve such cruel punishment and he cannot understand how God can let so much evil happen to a devotee like him, to someone so moral and honest.

Without losing his faith he longs to be justified before God and regain his honor as a righteous man. His words emanate from his heart with sincere faith: *Job 23:8-13 "If I go east, he is not there; if west, I can't find him; He works to the north, but I can't see him. He turns south, but I can't catch a glimpse of him. But he knows the way that I take. When he has tried me, I shall come forth like gold. My foot has held fast to his steps. I have kept his way, and not turned aside. I haven't gone back from the commandment of his lips. I have treasured up the words of his mouth more than my necessary food. But he stands alone, and who can oppose him? What his soul desires, even that he does."*

Job so desperately asks for an explanation of his so miserable state, the cause of it, applying – with unquestionable faith, innocence and sincerity – these questions to the One who holds all the answers. Job's friends cannot pacify his longing for justice since they superficially approach his questions. With a heart dry of true compassion and understanding, they merely use the traditional religious terms, devoid of deep contemplation and essential love. So indicative are the words of Job towards them *Job 13:4-5 "But you are forgers of lies. You are all physicians of no value. Oh that you would be completely silent! Then you would be wise."*

At this juncture, God appears and He responds to his faith, overwhelming him with a vision of His divine power and wisdom. He presents before his eyes the magnificence of the creation and the absolute harmony that has been poured for the genius design of all the creatures. A stream of continuous questions about the sacred secrets of the creation is addressed to Job. He really senses the grandeur of the Lord and replies with the following words: *Job 42:2-3 "I know that you can do all things, and that no purpose of yours can be restrained. You asked, 'Who is this who hides counsel without knowledge?' therefore I have uttered that which I did not understand, things too wonderful for me, which I didn't know."* Eventually Job is restored to his former condition, by the divine grace and bliss, with much more prosperity after this feverish trial of his faith. With extreme humbleness, which constitutes the core of the teachings of Jesus, he acknowledges the superiority of God, together with his own limitations to comprehend His vastness and the source of His wisdom: *Job 28:20-24 "Where then does wisdom come from? Where is the place of understanding? Seeing it is hidden from the eyes of all living, and kept close from the birds of the sky. Destruction and Death say, 'We have heard a rumor of it with our ears.' "God understands its way, and he knows its place. For he looks to the ends of the earth, and sees under the whole sky."*

Isaiah

Another great prophet who lives in Jerusalem in the latter half of the eighth century B.C. is Isaiah. The lack of trust people have in God, the human arrogance and pride, the futile performance of religious rituals for mere satisfaction of ego, characterize the period before the descent of Jesus. A divine shepherd comes to earth due to the ultimate compassion of God at those crucial periods when humankind has lost its connection with Him and needs to be guided and inspired to turn again towards Him and realize its divine nature and origin: *Isaiah 30:20-21 "Though the Lord may give you the bread of adversity and the water of affliction, yet your teachers won't be hidden anymore, but your eyes will see your teachers; and when you turn to the right hand, and when you turn to the left, your ears will hear a voice behind you, saying, 'This is the way. Walk in it.'"*

Isaiah spreads to people the message of regaining the connection with God, of living with justice and righteousness. He foretells the coming of Jesus and a time of a world-wide peace, where complete union dominates, where the One manifests in many. Describing the peaceful kingdom for those who will follow the rules of the great king, Jesus Christ, from the lineage of David, he expresses with such beautiful poetry the grandeur of Lord's kingdom: *Isaiah 11:6-10* "The wolf will live with the lamb, and the leopard will lie down with the young goat; The calf, the young lion, and the fattened calf together; and a little child will lead them. The cow and the bear will graze. Their young ones will lie down together. The lion will eat straw like the ox. The nursing child will play near a cobra's hole, and the weaned child will put his hand on the viper's den. They will not hurt nor destroy in all my holy mountain; for the earth will be full of the knowledge of the Lord, as the waters cover the sea. It will happen in that day that the nations will seek the root of Jesse, who stands as a banner of the peoples; and his resting place will be glorious."

Jeremiah and Hosea

A devotee to whom the word of the Lord is like fire in his heart is Jeremiah. He is a sensitive man who deeply loves his people, who speaks about the new covenant which will be written on the hearts of those who have burning faith to God. Jeremiah transfers with great emotion the divine call for inner transformation and tries to motivate people to reconsider their way of living: *Jeremiah 8:6-7* "[...] no man repents him of his wickedness, saying, 'What have I done?' Everyone turns to his course, as a horse that rushes headlong in the battle. Yes, the stork in the sky knows her appointed times; and the turtledove and the swallow and the crane observe the time of their coming; but my people don't know the Lord's law." Surrendering totally to the divine will, Jeremiah finds in Him the most reliable refuge and inspires all the sincere seekers to connect with the ultimate source of bliss, safety and prosperity: *Jeremiah 17:14 "Heal me, O Lord, and I shall be healed; save me, and I shall be saved: for you are my praise."* To all those who consciously try to reunite with this source and reestablish this connection, Lord transfers, through the poetic verses of Jeremiah, the following message: *Jeremiah 31:20-21 "[…] therefore my heart yearns for him; I will surely have mercy on him, says the Lord. Set up road signs, make guideposts; set your heart toward the highway, even the way by which you went […]"*

Similarly we meet in the words of prophet Hosea the truth and reliability of this everlasting love: *Hosea 14:4 "I will heal their waywardness. I will love them freely; for my anger is turned away from him."* The everlasting providence and grace of God provide the nectar of unquestioning faith and tremendous vigor for all those aspirants who are unceasingly challenged by adversities. These adversities are actually a boon, not a bane. Those who aim for nothing less than the eternal bliss, will have to be ever ready to tread the path of penance and renunciation, to live a pious life, as all the martyrs of the Christian tradition have done. No piety is greater than being the seeker of nothing but the ultimate truth. The realization of the divine is possible only in the inner-self, which has been sanctified by ascetic renunciation and it is driven by the sincere yearning for the ultimate truth.

Daniel

Prophet Daniel outlines the miraculous power of burning faith to the Lord. In the story of Daniel's three friends- Shadrach, Meshach and Abednego- who are sentenced to death due to their disobedience to the king- we witness this power. Unaffected by the fear of death, detached from the body consciousness and totally devoted to God, they receive the divine providence and although they are thrown into the blazing fire they show no sign of being hurt.

Dispelling the darkness of decay and death, through the light of incessant divine love, they transform the very essence of their physical body and go beyond its limitations and confinements: *Daniel 3:27 "The satraps, the deputies, and the governors, and the king's counselors, being gathered together, saw these men, that the fire had no power on their bodies, nor was the hair of their head singed, neither were their pants changed, nor had the smell of fire passed on them."* The inner blazing fire of devotion and constant love for the divine swallow the external flames and enable the devotees to attain miraculous supernatural abilities which reflect the subtle restoration of their primordial nature, where incorruptibility, immortality and divinization constitute its essence.

Jonah

The mercy of God and His supreme compassion for all His creatures is presented also in the book of Jonah whose breathtaking words emanate from the source of true devotional worship. When he is swallowed by a large fish, he remains for three days deep inside it and prays to the Lord, convinced that true salvation comes only through Him: *Jonah 2:9 "But I will sacrifice to you with the voice of thanksgiving. I will pay that which I have vowed. Salvation belongs to the Lord."* Then the Lord orders the fish to spit Jonah up on the beach and He reappears to remind him His ultimate compassion.

At an other part of the Old Testament, Jonah feels sorry when at God's command a worm attacks the plant which is offered to Jonah by God to give him some shade so that he would be more comfortable. Then God reveals to him how deep is His concern for His own children by using the following words indicative of His everlasting providence: *Jonah 4:10-11 "'Then said the Lord: 'You have been concerned for the vine, for which you have not labored, neither made it grow; which came up in a night, and perished in a night. Shouldn't I be concerned for Nineveh, that great city, in which are more than one hundred twenty thousand persons who can't discern between their right hand and their left hand; and also much livestock?'"* These compassionate divine words, travelling through the flute of prophet Jonah, pave the path for the ultimate revelation of God's compassion towards every single creature in this universe which takes place through the manifestation of Jesus Christ on earth. Jesus incarnates the divine Logos, being *Theanthropos*, and spreads to all the ultimate message of divinization, showing throughout His life the path towards it and making it accessible to each one of us.

Micah and Malachi

Prophet Micah is another bright example of a spiritual man who prepares the ground for Jesus' descent and discloses to all the people God's command *Micah 6:8 "He has shown you, O man, what is good. What does the Lord require of you, but to act justly, to love mercy, and to walk humbly with your God?"* His words, written hundreds of years before Jesus' manifestation on earth, are in complete harmony with His main message of service, selfless love and humbleness. Similarly at the last chapter of the Old Testament, prophet Malachi spreads the light of obedience to God's command and the certainty that the day of the Lord is coming: *Malachi 4:2 "But to you who fear my name shall the sun of righteousness arise with healing in its wings. You will go out, and leap like calves of the stall."*
All these prophets denote the message of Jesus' coming. Their undying faith to the divine scatters petals of feverish

devotion and love on the path where Christ will walk. The psalms, those mainly composed by David, seem to be the most appropriate music to accompany the holy descent of Jesus' that follows the preparation of all these prophets. The depths of these lyrics, as beautiful Cherubs, chants the glory of His name and invite all the devotees to live the life with Him.

Psalms 139:1-18

"Lord, you have searched me,
and you know me.
You know my sitting down and my rising up.
You perceive my thoughts from afar.
You search out my path and my lying down,
and are acquainted with all my ways.
For there is not a word on my tongue,
but, behold, Yahweh, you know it altogether.
You hem me in behind and before.
You laid your hand on me.
This knowledge is beyond me.
It's lofty.
I can't attain it.
Where could I go from your Spirit?
Or where could I flee from your presence?
If I ascend up into heaven, you are there.
If I make my bed in Sheolt, behold, you
are there!
If I take the wings of the dawn,
and settle in the uttermost parts of the
sea;
Even there your hand will lead me,
and your right hand will hold me.

If I say, "Surely the darkness will overwhelm me;
the light around me will be night";
even the darkness doesn't hide from you,
but the night shines as the day.
The darkness is like light to you.
For you formed my inmost being.
You knit me together in my mother's womb.
I will give thanks to you,
for I am fearfully and wonderfully made.
Your works are wonderful.
My soul knows that very well.
My frame wasn't hidden from you,
when I was made in secret,
woven together in the depths of the earth.
Your eyes saw my body.
In your book they were all written,
the days that were ordained for me,
when as yet there were none of them.
How precious to me are your thoughts, God!
How vast is their sum!
If I would count them, they are more in number than the sand.
When I wake up, I am still with you."

LORD'S DESCENT ON EARTH: THE IMMACULATE CONCEPTION OF JESUS CHRIST

Which other words could reflect more precisely and perfectly the descent of God through Jesus Christ than the first verses from the Gospel of John, where the grandeur of His miraculous birth breaks any sort of limitation and pours into the hearts of devotees, the first rays of His Light: *John 1:1-5 & 1:14 "In the beginning was the Word, and the Word was with God, and the Word was God. The same was in the beginning with God. All things were made through him. Without him was not anything made that has been made. In him was life, and the life was the light of men. The light shines in the darkness, and the darkness hasn't overcome it. [...] The Word became flesh, and lived among us. We saw his glory, such glory as of the one and only Son of the Father, full of grace and truth."* The Word, the Logos, the wisdom of God becomes flesh and assumes a physical form that is manifested through Jesus—the Theanthropos, as John the Baptist foretells: *John 1:15 "[...] This was he of whom I said, 'He who comes after me has surpassed me, for he was before me.'"*

Jesus Christ, the Son of God, moved by His supreme love and compassion for us, puts on our image, so that He will restore our nature, which has been entangled in the nets of the uttermost Hades. He intensely craves for the salvation of His children, so that they will be liberated, through His teachings, from the original sin that is the disconnection with Father and the resulting consequence of the mortality, of the venomous clutches of decay and death. For this purpose, His most high nature unites in a magnificent way with our human nature through All Holy Virgin Mary, who supplies Her own unsullied nature for His descent. Being absolutely spotless and pure, She is chosen to give human nature to the Word of God.

The Holy Ground of His conception: All Holy Virgin Mary

Ever-Virgin Mary, the holy mother of Jesus, becomes the sacred land for His immaculate conception and physical manifestation on earth, having the fullness of divine grace prior to the conception, during the conception and after the conception of Jesus Christ. Encountering the celestial beauty of Her life[2], we clearly understand why She is selected to be '*Theotokos*', which means in Greek language 'the one who has given birth to God'.

Her virtuous parents, Joachim and Anna, praying for an end to their childlessness, promise that if a child is born to them, they will offer it back to the Giver, they will dedicate it to the service of God. When the All Holy Virgin reaches the age of three, the pious parents decide to fulfill their vow and take Her to the holy temple of Jerusalem. There the High Priest, Zacharias, and other priests meet the Ever- Holy Mary, the precious handmaiden of God. In the Temple, fifteen high steps lead to the sanctuary, which only the priests and High Priest can enter. Just as they place Her on the first step, empowered

---

[2] *Saint Gregory Palamas' writing "Discourse on the feast of the entry of our most pure lady Theotokos into the Holy of the Holies" is a precious source of information about Holy Virgin Mary's life, giving us an incredible insight into Her mystical life.*

by the Holy Spirit, She quickly goes up the remaining steps of the temple and ascends to the highest one.

Then the High Priest, inspired from this marvelous incident, leads the All Holy Virgin into the Holy of Holies, where only he is authorized to enter once every year to offer a purifying sacrifice of blood. The Holy of the Holies is destined only for those who have reached *theosis* (divinization). It is the innermost sanctuary of the temple, out of sight of almost everyone and protected by walls and curtains. All Holy Virgin Mary takes this place, which is assigned to God alone, as Her home and resides there preserved only from God. The Holy Maid, alone of mankind, detached from all the worldly delights while still an infant, is nourished directly from heaven by an angel, by which she is physically empowered. Her celestial nourishment is a clear testimony that her way of life was heavenly. She is sustained by the divine grace, in order to become capable of containing divinity itself, so that the mystery of God's incarnation can take place through Her.

The All Pure Virgin, following a pious way of life being in absolute solitude, is enjoying constantly the divine company, love and providence. She prays unceasingly in sacred quiet from such early childhood, contemplating upon God with holy stillness. Having remained until the age of Her puberty in the Holy of the Holies inside the temple, She reaches the Holy of the Holies of the spiritual life, She reaches illumination and *theosis*. In this manner, Holy Virgin Mary, the queen of the holy pious, is virgin in the body and in the soul.

Through the pure channel of Holy Virgin Mary Lord manifests receiving all the required gross elements in order to exist among the people, teach them and inspire them to return to Life, to overcome death literally and experience His kingdom at every level with no bondage. The birth of Jesus, of the Messiah, takes place after fourteen generations from Abraham to David, fourteen generations from David to the exile in Babylon and another fourteen generations since then. Joseph, who marries Holy Virgin Mary, is the last ancestor of his generation and a descendant of David. Through the Gospels of Jesus' disciples we receive glorious glimpses of His descent on earth and we witness the revelation, at gross and physical level, of the formless divine consciousness which is eternal, beyond time, space and causality. The divine formless power takes flesh and blood and each cell of the apparent physical body of Jesus vibrates the Word, God Himself, and serves with total commitment the ultimate goal for which each one has been shaped under God's command.

It is very important to note at this point that the path for His arrival is opened through His most faithful servant, John the Baptist. Specifically, six months before the appearance of the angel Gabriel to the Holy Virgin Mary to announce Jesus' birth through Her, the angel Gabriel visits Zechariah and informs him that although his wife Elizabeth is very old still she will give birth to John who will be great in the Lord's eyes: *Luke 1:13-16 "But the angel said to him, "Don't be afraid, Zacharias, because your request has been heard, and your wife, Elizabeth, will bear you a son, and you shall call his name John. You will have joy and gladness; and many will rejoice at his birth. For he will be great in the sight of the Lord, and he will drink no wine nor strong drink. He will be filled with the Holy Spirit, even from his mother's womb. He will turn many of the children of Israel to the Lord, their God."* Initially Zechariah does not believe the angel's message and Gabriel informs him that he will remain silent until the day his promise to him is fulfilled.

During the sixth month of Elizabeth's pregnancy God sends the angel Gabriel to Nazareth carrying this message to Holy Virgin Mary, promised in marriage to a man named

Joseph: *Luke 1:30-33 "The angel said to her, 'Don't be afraid, Mary, for you have found favor with God. Behold, you will conceive in your womb, and bring forth a son, and will call his name 'Jesus.' He will be great, and will be called the Son of the Most High. The Lord God will give him the throne of his father, David, and he will reign over the house of Jacob forever. There will be no end to his Kingdom.'"* Holy Virgin Mary wonders how is it possible to be pregnant since She is virgin and Gabriel answers that the Holy Spirit has actually come on Her and God's power will rest upon Her. The angel asks Her to remember Her relative, Elizabeth, who is also six months pregnant despite her old age and soon afterwards Holy Virgin Mary visits Elizabeth: *Luke 1:41-45 "It happened, when Elizabeth heard Mary's greeting, that the baby leaped in her womb, and Elizabeth was filled with the Holy Spirit. She called out with a loud voice, and said, 'Blessed are you among women, and blessed is the fruit of your womb! Why am I so favored, that the mother of my Lord should come to me? For behold, when the voice of your greeting came into my ears, the baby leaped in my womb for joy! Blessed is she who believed, for there will be a fulfillment of the things which have been spoken to her from the Lord!'"*

On the day of the annunciation, when the Good News is announced, through the archangel—spreading the message that the Logos of the Almighty will be incarnated for man's salvation—Holy Virgin Mary receives the Holy Spirit. Her response to the message of the archangel that she is granted to give birth to Christ indicates and lucidly expresses Her divine state: *Luke 1:38 "Mary said, 'Behold, the handmaid of the Lord; be it to me according to your word.'"* Her obedience to the words of the archangel and her commitment to God's command, for an event that is so odd for normal human logic, shows clearly that Her logic is totally submitted to God's will.

Having uttermost purity and absolute faith, She is perfectly qualified to serve as an efficient carrier of His divine descent, manifested in flesh and blood.

At the same time Joseph who is engaged to Holy Virgin Mary, learning that She is pregnant and is going to have a child by the Holy Spirit, doesn't want to disgrace Her publicly and so he decides to break the engagement privately. Yet the appearance of an angel in his dreams confirms that what is said through the prophets comes true: *Matthew 1:22-23 "Now all this has happened, that it might be fulfilled which was spoken by the Lord through the prophet, saying, 'Behold, the virgin shall be with child, and shall bring forth a son. They shall call his name Immanuel'; which is, being interpreted, 'God with us.'"*"and this vision inspires Joseph to marry Holy Virgin Mary. He takes active part during the unfolding of the divine plan. He initially seems very surprised about what is happening to him, yet the presence of God through His angel calms his heart as a balsam. Finally, he also feels inspired to follow with unquestioning faith the Lord's command, ignoring all the rituals and the social prejudices of that period.

The spiritual grandeur and innocence of Holy Virgin Mary and the obedience of Joseph to follow God's command with no doubt, purify the channel through which the divinity will descend to earth in order to guide people and strengthen their belief that eternal life is possible, literally. This is possible only when one demolishes his ego and dives deeply into the divine ocean, with complete surrender and self-annihilation. Holy Virgin Mary is qualified, because of Her inner purity and innocence, to be in harmony with the descent of the divine. Due to Her inwards focus and feverish faith, She is granted to experience the flow of divine consciousness in Her physical body which pours supreme bliss and joy to Her.

The uniqueness of Jesus' Immaculate Conception

The immaculate conception of Jesus is fulfilled through an extraordinary process, which is in no way comparable to the normal standards. As a divine incarnation Jesus can enter into the womb of a mother directly by His grace with no other medium or carrier as the semen of man. It would be really enlightening to observe carefully the uniqueness of this miraculous conception of Jesus Christ. Normally the process of conception and resultant pregnancy includes the following three basic phases:

a) Ovulation: Each month, in one of a woman's two ovaries, a group of immature eggs start to develop in small fluid-filled cysts called follicles. Normally, one of the follicles is selected to complete development (maturation). The mature follicle ruptures and releases the egg from the ovary (ovulation).

b) Fertilization: A great number of sperms are released in the ovary during the process of copulation. If one of the sperms does meet and penetrate a mature egg after ovulation, that will fertilize it. At the moment of fertilization, the baby's genetic make-up is complete, including its sex.

c) Implantation: Within 24-hours after fertilization, the egg begins dividing rapidly into many cells. The fertilized egg becomes a solid ball of cells, and then it becomes a hollow ball of cells called a blastocyst. Within three weeks, the blastocyst cells begin to grow as clumps of cells within that little ball, and the baby's first nerve cells have already formed. The developing baby is called an embryo from the moment of conception to the eighth week of pregnancy. After the eighth week and until the moment of birth, the developing baby is called a fetus.

The conception of Jesus Christ happens through an absolutely unique process. Normally the sperm, carrying the life-force, lightens the spark of conception inside an ovary for every ordinary being that is limited by every means: physical, mental, intellectual. But in the case of Jesus' conception, the circumstances are completely different. Here, Jesus, the limitless divine consciousness, the Logos Itself, being so grand and expansive, does not need such a physical medium in order to descend. Sperm carries an unconscious and undeveloped existence with certain limitations but the Logos is the absolute consciousness, carrying three fundamental divine qualities: omnipresence, omniscience and omnipotence. Still, as sunrays cannot come directly on earth and need to be filtered, similarly for the sake of the physical manifestation of these qualities, they have to be covered and be revealed gradually throughout the life of Jesus. While He is manifesting them, filtered on the gross level, He is opening the path for all of us to connect essentially with them and experience the divinity that lies within us, still in latent form. How beautifully Prophet David foretells about His conception in the womb of Holy Mother: *Psalms 72:6 "He will come down like rain on the mown grass, as showers that water the earth."* Just as rain comes down on the grass without causing any noise, similarly, the descent of Jesus inside the womb of Holy Virgin Mary is so quiet and blissful that does not create any corruption to Her virginity and spotless purity.

Thus, no physical medium is required and the descent takes place directly inside the body of Holy Virgin Mary. She becomes the most appropriate ground for this descent since She has already been liberated from all the gross confinements owing to Her pious life and austere practice. Living constantly for many years inside the temple of Jerusalem- being the only person who can have direct access in this holy ground - She has reached in such spiritual height that even gross nutrition is not necessary for Her. As we saw above, at a very tender young age of Her life, by chanting incessantly God's name inside the temple, She receives directly the ambrosia from angels. The innermost purity and uttermost innocence blossom within Her during these years and She is granted to accept such a precious power. This divine power enables Her to carry within Her the Son of God, Jesus Christ. She is the deserving one who can receive and assimilate this divine nutrition that carries immense energy. Her transformed physical body and this accumulated divine nutrition constitute the soil that accepts the Seed of life, the unmanifested divine consciousness.

Examining carefully the process of this immaculate conception, we notice that the three typical stages of ovulation, fertilization and implantation, which constitute the essence of a normal conception, follow a divine route for the virgin birth of Jesus. His immaculate conception breaks all the limitations of these normal stages and reflects the divinity of this birth. At the stage of ovulation, Holy Virgin Mary is actually the special chosen 'follicle' among all the rest, so completely developed and mature that can be the womb of Life. Her oceanic devotion to God and continuous prayer grant Her with the honorable selection for this mission, since She is above all the physical limitations and the divine light is prevalent inside Her.

At the stage of fertilization, through Her womb, the link between kingdom of heaven and earth is established since God, in the form of Jesus Christ, consciously approaches Her womb and blesses it with His presence. His descent pervades Holy Virgin Mary, becoming an immanent part inside Her. Still, it is very necessary to clarify at this point that Jesus' conception is totally independent from the need of copulation since it is not a product or a result of such an activity. Jesus descends due to His ultimate compassion for the humankind. Humans have been entangled inside the nets of the original sin, of passions, delusions and worldly attractions and are condemned to mortality. He manifests in order to uplift the humankind from this perishable and pitiful state. He appears to guide them, through His life, towards the highest state of immortality. He comes down to the gross level of the humankind obtaining a physical form, in order to help them elevate and be liberated from the original sin.

At the stage of implantation, as we have noticed also at the stage of fertilization, there is actually no necessity of gradual development since Jesus is descending being already absolutely perfect. The words of Saint John Damascene are indicative: *"At the moment of flesh, at that moment the flesh of God the Word"*. This means that there is no interval of time, after the conception, for the human nature of Jesus Christ to be divinized, but this happens immediately at the time He is conceived. However, in order to be linked with this gross level of humankind and unfold the divine plan, He assumes an individual form and His perfection is covered, apparently yet not essentially, by physical layers. Everything exists inside Him in seed form, still for the sake of the service to humanity everything is revealed gradually. This manifestation of His inherent divinity reaches to the pinnacle through His Resurrection, through His complete transformation to an immortal body. To convey the message of the ultimate divine metamorphosis and to teach the ordinary people, He exhibits throughout His life all His supernatural powers, which reside within Him, in seed form, since His immaculate conception. Eventually, the crescendo of this gradual manifestation is fulfilled with His victory upon the last, the ultimate enemy, the death. God manifests in flesh and blood through Jesus, the formless takes shape and form, in order to be physically accessible and guide all the beings on the inner path of ultimate evolution. Right from inside the womb His glory radiates and inspires the devotees. Elizabeth, venerated mother of John the Baptist, is a witness of this extraordinary pregnancy. When Holy Virgin Mary visits Elizabeth during the sixth month of Her pregnancy, Elizabeth is overwhelmed by the intense inrush of the Holy Spirit within her. Experiencing this transcendental state, the truth about the existence of Messiah inside the womb of Holy Virgin Mary is revealed to her. Inspired from this realization she conveys a very lucid message to Holy Mother of Jesus, saying to Her that She is the most blessed among all the women, carrying within Her such blessed fruit, the son of God, the magnanimous Lord.

Holy Virgin Mary is able to decipher the divine message of immaculate conception due to her purity and innocence and resultantly She decides, with full awareness, to sacrifice Herself. She surrenders completely to the divine will with no resistance or doubt. Those devotees who follow Holy Virgin Mary's devotional path will be granted equally to experience in totality within themselves the birth of Jesus Christ. They will even imbibe this experience at a physical level. The birth of Jesus Christ will actually take place within them, it will not be experienced separately from them. The nectar of divine consciousness will imbue each one of their cells and it will penetrate every knot or blockage. This nectar will 'eat' the grossness of the physical body and a new birth of an immortalized body will reflect the implantation of Logos and the complete divine transformation in every level, even the gross one. In the case of Holy Virgin Mary, Her womb becomes the ground for the manifestation of Jesus on earth. Accordingly, in the case of the sincere devotees who tread the path of the true spiritual lineage of Jesus, their whole body will become the actual womb for His manifestation. The total body of the aspirant, who has been enlightened from the ultimate call of Jesus towards perfection and sanctification, is the womb where Jesus reveals all His Glory. Each cell of this transformed and immortalized body is offered as the soil for the divine descent and each single cell as a sanctuary praises the Lord, spreading the celestial music of Prophet David's verse: *Psalms 150:6 "Let everything that has breath praise the Lord! Praise the Lord!"*

John the Baptist

John the Baptist is 'the voice of one crying out in the wilderness': *"Make ready the way of the Lord. Make his paths straight"*, in accord to the words of prophet Isaiah as it is mentioned at the *Gospel of Matthew 3:3*. John the Baptist, being the most authentic example of a disciple, foretells with extreme humbleness to all that Jesus is the lamb of God, the Messiah, the Savior. He is the one who will spiritually guide everyone who seeks to accomplish salvation from all the worldly sufferings and regain his inherent eternal peace and bliss: *Matthew 3:11 "I indeed baptize you in water for repentance, but he who comes after me is mightier than I, whose sandals I am not worthy to carry. He will baptize you in the Holy Spirit."* Jesus is the manifestation of divine amongst the people in a form accessible to their abilities and John the Baptist has the mission to spread the message of this divine manifestation.

When Holy Virgin Mary and Her relative Elizabeth meet each other we watch the miracle of the divine plan. John the Baptist denotes his existence and makes his mother aware of it. While Holy Virgin Mary greets Elizabeth, John the Baptist within the womb of his mother jumps from gladness and Elizabeth salutes Her as her Lord's mother. Mary sings the praise to Lord: *Luke 1:46-50 "Mary said, 'My soul magnifies the Lord. My spirit has rejoiced in God my Savior, for he has looked* at the humble state of his handmaid. *For behold, from now on, all generations will call me blessed. For he who is mighty has done great things for me. Holy is his name. His mercy is for generations of generations on those who fear him."* Holy Virgin Mary stays close to Elizabeth for three months and then goes back to Her home. The birth of John the Baptist takes place and Zechariah confirming the name that shall be given to this child is enabled to speak again and praise the glory of God. He recognizes the special mission of his child and informs all others of the grand path which John the Baptist will tread in his life: *Luke 1:76-79 "And you, child, will be called a prophet of the Most High, for you will go before the face of the Lord to prepare his ways, to give knowledge of salvation to his people by the remission of their sins, because of the tender mercy of our God, whereby the dawn from on high will visit us, to shine on those who sit in darkness and the shadow of death; to guide our feet into the way of peace."*

THE BIRTH OF
JESUS CHRIST AND THE
FIRST YEARS OF HIS LIFE

As different pieces of a jigsaw puzzle join harmoniously with each other to form a complete picture, similarly every part of Jesus' life- from the initial stage of His immaculate conception till the ultimate stage of His Resurrection- join with each other perfectly and successively reveal the vast picture of His descent and mission on earth. Divine arrangements prepare so wisely the ground for His manifestation, outlining the special descent of Messiah. As glorious has been His immaculate conception, equally marvelous and illustrious is His birth, declaring lucidly the exclusiveness of His presence on earth.

Holy Virgin Mary and Joseph, these loyal servants of God, unravel the divine plan with total faith and devotion. At that period, just before Jesus' birth, Emperor Augustus orders a census to be taken throughout the Roman Empire. Thus Joseph, along with expecting Holy Virgin Mary, travels from Nazareth to his hometown, Bethlehem where Herod is the king, in order to register himself. It is here Jesus Christ is born, verifying the truth of prophet's words: *Matthew 2:6 "You Bethlehem, land of Judah, are in no way least among the princes of Judah: for out of you shall come forth a governor, who shall shepherd my people, Israel."* Due to the census, many people have crowded together in Bethlehem, thus it is impossible for Joseph and

Holy Virgin Mary to find an available room in the inn of the city. We assume that Holy Virgin Mary gives birth to Jesus in open air. How could it be otherwise for the Son of God, for the Theanthropos? Only the ground of mother nature, being as vast and magnanimous as Him, could give shelter for the birth of Messiah. Nature seems to be the most appropriate place for the manifestation of the selected One, the One who incarnates God in flesh and blood and belongs to not a single one but everyone: *Luke 2:7 "She brought forth her firstborn son, and she wrapped him in bands of cloth, and laid him in a feeding trough, because there was no room for them in the inn."* The Lamb of God, Jesus Christ, who is meant to become the guide of all those who seek to be reunited with God and who will sacrifice Himself for the benefit of all, finds now a tender shelter in a manger. How beautiful are all the divine arrangements to glorify the humbleness and simplicity of Jesus, virtues that constitute the gist of His teachings! The absolute ruler, the one who has the total authority in the kingdom of heaven, the king of the kings finds shelter in the most simple and ordinary place, indicating the actual wealth, the authentic royalty, which is nothing else than the everlasting connection with the supreme God.

The Glory of Jesus' Birth

In that part of Bethlehem some shepherds are informed, through the appearance of an angel, about the birth of Lord: *Luke 2:10-12 "The angel said to them, "Don't be afraid, for behold, I bring you good news of great joy which will be to all the people. For there is born to you, this day, in the city of David, a Savior, who is Christ the Lord. This is the sign to you: you will find a baby wrapped in strips of cloth, lying in a feeding trough."* This angel is accompanied by a great army of heaven's angels who chant celestial praises for God. The shepherds, inspired from the message of the angel, decide to search for the Messiah and eventually find Him lying in the manger. They inform Holy Virgin Mary about their visions and it puts her into deep contemplation. The appearance of the angel and the celestial sounds of the heavenly angels that accompany him clearly indicate how unique and unrivalled is the birth of Jesus, how perfectly everything has been arranged to reveal His descent.

Meanwhile, Herod learns the exact time of Jesus' birth with the help of some visitors from East who are able to study the stars. Being extremely worried for his kingdom, Herod desperately seeks to find the child who is supposed to be the king of the Jews according to the prophecies and instructs these visitors to make a careful search for the child: *Matthew 2:9-12 "They, having heard the king, went their way; and behold, the star, which they saw in the east, went before them, until it came and stood over where the young child was. When they saw the star, they rejoiced with exceedingly great joy. They came into the house and saw the young child with Mary, his mother, and they fell down and worshiped him. Opening their treasures, they offered to him gifts: gold, frankincense, and myrrh. Being warned in a dream that they shouldn't return to Herod, they went back to their own country another way."* As in the sky, the seven stars of the Big Dipper always point the Polaris, the guiding star that marks always the way due north, similarly the star above the manger points the three visitors towards Jesus, the divine *Pole Star*. Jesus is indeed the steadfast *Pole Star* that guides and directs all the sincere seekers towards the everlasting source of wisdom and eternal bliss. His divine light spreads myriads of rays carrying His compassionate guidance all around, orientating all the travelers towards the infinite divine journey. He is the *Polaris*, the unique radiant star that lightens the path for all those who sail in the vast ocean of God, for all those who study carefully the divine sky and seek guidance from it.

Surrendering to God's command

An angel appears again in a dream to Joseph and instructs him to leave Bethlehem, taking the mother and the child along and escape to Egypt. This new message comes due to the fact that Herod, irritated by learning that the visitors from East have returned to their country from another road – since God warns them through a dream to not go back to Herod – gives orders to kill all the boys in Bethlehem until the age of two years, confirming the words of prophet Jeremiah: *Matthew 2:18 "A voice was heard in Ramah, lamentation, weeping and great mourning, Rachel weeping for her children; she wouldn't be comforted, because they are no more."* A little later, Joseph and Holy Virgin Mary, along with Christ, return from Egypt after learning that Herod is dead and go to the town of Nazareth, a city which will be blessed from now on with the presence of Jesus and observe Him grow.

It is very important to note, at this point, the absence of personal will behind any action of Joseph and Holy Virgin Mary. They have offered their minds at the feet of the Lord and each of their steps emanates from divine counseling. The purity of their hearts, unquestioning faith and firm determination motivate them to walk with steadfast devotion the precious path that God has granted them. Their total commitment to the divine will qualifies them to have this harmonious communication with God and experience directly the inner guidance and counseling, through angels of God who reveal to them His will. They are certain in their hearts that as long as they obey the divine command with total faith there is no space for misery, worry or insecurity. Joseph and Holy Virgin Mary offer unconditionally their service to the child who they sincerely believe is the Messiah and not an ordinary child. They are willing to face any adversity in order to serve their Lord and eager to make any sacrifice, even to go against the social norms of their time if required, so that they can perform perfectly this great task that has been applied to them by God.

The time comes for Joseph and Holy Virgin Mary to perform the ceremony of purification as the Law of Moses has commanded. So they take Jesus in the temple of Jerusalem to present Him to the Lord as it is written in the law that *"Every first-born male is to be dedicated to the Lord"* and offer also the required sacrifices. Simeon, a very pious man, also visits the temple that day. The Holy Spirit lives within him and has assured him that he would not die unless he will see the Lord's promised Messiah. When Simeon takes the child in his lap he says: *Luke 2:29-32 "Now you are releasing your servant, Master, according to your word, in peace; for my eyes have seen your salvation, which you have prepared before the face of all peoples; a light for revelation to the nations, and the glory of your people Israel."* Simeon, due to his spiritual advanced level, is able to recognize the descent of God through this special child and sees in Jesus His real essence beyond time, space and causality. With clear discrimination and a burning craving to meet the Messiah he is blessed to have awareness about the true nature of Jesus Christ beyond His present physical form. Simeon blesses His parents and foretells to Holy Virgin Mary that deep sorrow, like a sharp sword, will break Her heart, since many will speak against Him revealing their evil thoughts and oppose the truths that He, a sign of God to this world, will teach.

Jesus at the temple of Jerusalem

Luke 2:40 "The child was growing, and was becoming strong in spirit, being filled with wisdom, and the grace of God was upon him." At the age of twelve, Jesus together with Joseph and Holy Virgin Mary, visit again Jerusalem for the Passover festival – the Jewish Easter. After the festival they take the way back to Nazareth, unaware of the fact that Jesus doesn't accompany the group and has stayed back at the temple of Jerusalem. Eventually they realize His absence and after three days of searching they find Jesus sitting with the Jewish teachers and discussing with them. He is asking them extremely intelligent questions and He is giving also brilliant answers to their questions. All who are present in the temple are really amazed with the wisdom and inner wealth of this young boy: *Luke 2:48-50 "When they saw him, they were astonished, and his mother said to him, 'Son, why have you treated us this way? Behold, your father and I were anxiously looking for you.' He said to them, 'Why were you looking for me? Didn't you know that I must be in my Father's house?' They didn't understand the saying which he spoke to them."*

Jesus Christ fully aware of His origin, of His true identity and totally free from any sort of attachment or fear reveals the first rays of His supreme condition. Owing to His sharp discrimination and continuous connection with the ultimate divine source, He recognizes His origin and finds shelter at His Father's house. As a true seeker, He asks the truth from the spiritual teachers and impresses them with the depth of His questions. At the age of twelve, we meet Jesus in a state of pure focus and of sincere dispassion for worldly attractions. He seeks nothing else than the truth. After this incident, Jesus goes back with Mary and Joseph to Nazareth: *Luke 2:51-52 "And he went down with them, and came to Nazareth. He was subject to them, and his mother kept all these sayings in her heart. And Jesus increased in wisdom and stature, and in favor with God and men."*

THE BAPTISM AND THE
TEMPTATION OF JESUS CHRIST

The Baptism of Jesus Christ with the Holy Spirit

After the last incident in the temple of Jerusalem, we have no other information from the New Testament about Jesus' young years. We meet Him again at the age of thirty coming from Galilee in Bethany, on the east side of the Jordan River, where John the Baptist is baptizing people. Living in the desert and practicing extremely hard spiritual austerities, John the Baptist is unceasingly calling people to repentance and he is foretelling the descent of Messiah who is coming to guide the people and make them realize that they are actually an inseparable part of God. When Jesus arrives before John in order to be baptized as all the rest of the people, John, recognizing Him, asks with supreme humility to baptize him instead: *Matthew 3:15 "But Jesus, answering, said to him, "Allow it now, for this is the fitting way for us to fulfill all righteousness." Then he allowed him."*

Literally, the prophecy of John the Baptist that he is merely baptizing people with water, while Jesus will baptize with the Holy Spirit, is fulfilled when Jesus comes out of the Jordan River: *Mark 1:10-11 "Immediately coming up from the water, he saw the heavens parting, and the Spirit descending on him like a dove. A voice came out of the sky, 'You are my beloved Son, in whom I am well pleased.'"* The time for the revelation of the Messiah has come and the descent of the Holy

Spirit indicates the arrival of this moment. The Holy Spirit spreads the vibes of His celestial presence all around. As the sun cannot stay covered for long by the clouds as its radiant rays ultimately disperse them, similarly the everlasting Holy Spirit that resides in Jesus, from His immaculate conception, is eventually unlocked and descends to the gross level before the eyes of the masses. The Holy Spirit, indicating the innermost peace of Jesus' souls, manifests externally and introduces the presence of Messiah amongst the people. Jesus Christ becomes the open channel through which people can have a direct link to God and experience the bliss of His kingdom. God is pleased with Jesus who reflects perfectly the divine presence at every level of His being and expresses to Him, His prosperity. He confirms that now Jesus is eligible to guide the humanity since He is His beloved Son who is meant to be the eternal Savior, the compassionate Messiah. During all the past years Jesus is unceasingly united with the Holy Spirit being prepared for Its descent. Now the time has come for the manifestation of the Holy Spirit before the eyes of the crowds and Jesus is unraveling the divine plan, in total commitment to God's will.

Forty days in the desert

Luke 4:1-2 *"Jesus, full of the Holy Spirit, returned from the Jordan, and was led by the Spirit into the wilderness for forty days, being tempted by the devil. He ate nothing in those days. Afterward, when they were completed, he was hungry."* After His baptism and the flow of the Holy Spirit through each cell of His totality that is witnessed even at the gross level, Jesus spends forty days in isolation, in the desert facing various temptations from the Devil. The purity of His mind enables Him to endure and overcome all these temptations. This purity, austerity and endurance eventually transform His physical body to such an extent that it becomes free from any external dependence. Being unceasingly united with the source of the primordial energy inside, the energy that pervades and sustains everything, He becomes totally independent and self sufficient.

At this juncture, it is important to note that such periods of isolation in desert carry a great significance for those divine personalities who wish to listen solely to God's voice. As we see in the case of Jesus, of Moses, of John the Baptist, the practice of solitude, accompanied with austerities and incessant glorification of God, provides the appropriate ground for the direct communication with God. This absolute disconnection from anything worldly, this total emptiness and independence is necessary in order to receive with flawless focus the divine message and experience the descent of God's grace and guidance within them. Additionally, it is remarkable to observe that such periods of isolation endure forty days, in most of the cases. The notable fact that these solitudes last always the same number of days naturally makes us wonder if there is a special significance for this particular duration. Nevertheless, we clearly understand from all these cases that isolation is extremely important practice for all those devotees who are granted and are eligible to enjoy exclusively the veracious companion of their souls, God Himself.

Freedom from external dependences

During these forty days of isolation in desert, where no external supply is available, Jesus stays totally disconnected from the outer world and free from all the external means, practicing extremely austere fasting. The fact that He is free from any sort of external dependence, during this period of His solitude, gives a clear evidence that He receives divine nourishment directly from God. The sole purpose of His solitude is the direct communication with God and with this one-pointed focus, He disregards any need for His physical body. His exclusive focus is for the divine. Why would He care about any physical provision in such a state? Being totally concentrated on this divine contact and so introverted, all His senses are turned inwards and the flow of divine energy is rushing inside Him with extreme force as an impetuous torrent. Thus, there is absolute independency, something which we have already encountered in Old Testament in the case of Moses. Jesus and Moses spend exactly equal number of days in the desert under the same circumstances. Owing to their ultimate connection with God and absolute dependence on Him, they break all the physical limitations and are nourished by this divine nectar. God is taking care of all their needs for their survival. How clearly Jesus states later on to His disciples the presence of this everlasting divine nourishment *John 4:31-32 "In the meanwhile, the disciples urged him, saying, 'Rabbi, eat.' But he said to them, 'I have food to eat that you don't know about.'"*

Jesus discovers this divine nectar, this precious gift from God during His isolation in desert. As it is natural for a true Shepherd, He shares the discovery of this celestial provision with His flock. Moreover, owing to His unparallel concern and compassion, He teaches the exact path through which all can have access to this divine nourishment. Beyond words is His love and providence for all of us, a love similar to the vast sky, which gives its shelter to all and wants nothing in return. Later, during Lord's Supper we will see Him not just mentioning but also calling His students to taste this divine nectar and go beyond any worldly dependence: *Matthew 26:29 "But I tell you that I will not drink of this fruit of the vine from now on, until that day when I drink it a new with you in my Father's Kingdom."*

Jesus, being totally liberated from any worldly means, rises beyond physicality and becomes one with the inner source that is in direct contact with the Ultimate, with God. Every gross bondage and confinement is dispelled by the light of the divine energy that oozes within Jesus who is the bread of Life, as He calls Himself at the *Gospel of John 6:35 "Jesus said to them, "I am the bread of life. He who comes to me will not be hungry, and he who believes in me will never be thirsty."* His physical body becomes the chariot of divine grace on earth and a direct link with the Creator. He is inviting all of us to be a part of His Supper, to enjoy this ambrosia and nectar: *Luke 22:29-30 "I confer on you a kingdom, even as my Father conferred on me, that you may eat and drink at my table in my Kingdom. You will sit on thrones, judging the twelve tribes of Israel."* Apparently, we may not be the kings, however, we certainly have the heritage of Kingdom of Heaven from the Lord and we are granted with His everlasting compassionate guidance "*now and ever and to ages of ages*", as so beautifully is chanted at the Thrice Holy Hymn.

Jesus, completely aware of His reality, His divine origin and the fact that the Kingdom of Heaven lies within, is in perfect tune with the inner source of life, the all-pervading God. This inner connection nourishes and energizes Him, therefore, no external means is required for His survival. On the contrary, things are entirely different for us. Being entangled inside the nets of the worldly attractions, all our senses and the nine orifices that are related to these senses (eyes, nostrils, ears, mouth, genitals and anus) run forcefully outwards, mesmerized from the glitter and glory of this world. Owing to this outwards focus, we gradually disconnect from the eternal source of life and resultantly our inner strength diminishes. Being so much extroverted, we are not able to imbibe the divine energy appropriately. Thus, we depend mainly on the gross food for sustenance, which further adds to the grossness of our physical body and causes cluttering inside. This cluttering does not allow divine energy to touch the deeper levels and assimilate efficiently. Instead, Jesus Christ is able to imbibe directly the vibrating form of energy owing to the divinity of His personality and constant inner connection. Conclusively, the certain fact that we are still devoid of this divine nourishment indicates our disconnection with the ultimate source of this energy and the necessity to reunite with it in full awareness and consciousness, following with all our heart, mind, strength and soul the path that Jesus has paved for us. Undoubtedly, Jesus has opened the way for us that leads directly to the divine, to the eternal life. Now we have to check ourselves attentively and see clearly – where we stand, what impediments are blocking our way and how far we stand from our ultimate predestination—the manifestation of our inherent divinity.

The first appearance of tempter

Jesus Christ pierces through His prayer and austerities every single knot obstructing the inner connection and by the light of manifestation of His divine nature: He disperses the shadow of ignorance, which is actually the tempter *Matthew 4:3-4 "The tempter came and said to him, 'If you are the Son of God, command that these stones become bread.' But he answered, 'It is written, 'Man shall not live by bread alone, but by every word that proceeds out of the mouth of God.'"* The Devil, the Satan is actually the ignorance, the shadow of light and knowledge. Those aspirants who turn their face completely towards God and annihilate themselves by devoting each iota of their existence to the glory of His name, experience the forces of the tempter and for them there is the danger of falling. The closer one is going towards the light, the grander becomes the shadow that is formed behind him, thus greater becomes the power of the forces of ignorance to prevent the unrolling of true knowledge and self realization.

Those who sincerely aspire to meet the Lord may have great falls due to these forces, which pull all the senses outwards. On the other side, the people who are on the ground, who are entangled in the veils of materialism and outward focus, have actually no fear to fall. The danger of falling exists for those who try to fly, to rise above body consciousness, to break the limitations of grossness and physicality. And certainly there is no danger for those who serve such forces by fulfilling their demands and quests.

Jesus is challenged to lose His unquestioning trust to God's hands and, as Adam and Eve, to commit the sin of replacing His providence. He is asked to misuse His miraculous powers in order to please His sensual needs. Jesus with firm determination and crystal-clear focus – owing to His direct contact with the inner source – remains unaffected by this temptation. He knows that God will take care of all His needs and He considers any personal selfish effort sinful as it would actually signify His lack of faith in God: *Matthew 6:31-33 "Therefore don't be anxious, saying, 'What will we eat?', 'What will we drink?' or, 'With what will we be clothed?' For the Gentiles seek after all these things; for your heavenly Father knows that you need all these things. But seek first God's Kingdom, and his righteousness; and all these things will be given to you as well."* The miraculous powers from the Holy Spirit are not meant to be manifested for His own pleasure but to fulfill the much higher spiritual mission. Whenever miracles are performed, they emanate from the ultimate compassion of God for all His children and strengthen the seed of their faith and determination to walk on the divine path.

The actual meaning of hunger

At this point it is essential to analyze further the deepest meaning of hunger. The root cause of the hunger, let that be for gross food, for name and fame, for sensual enjoyment, for any sort of outer expectation is one: the ignorance of our true nature. Jesus realizes the root of hunger during this period of absolute disconnection from any external source. He realizes the ignorance and He senses the actual 'hunger' before His absolute victory over all the forces which pull down one's consciousness and limit the expansion of understanding. The tempter actually challenges Him to raise His ego, to be entangled inside the nets of ignorance and identification with the physical body. However, Jesus during this period of complete isolation, being directly connected with the inner source, the Kingdom of Heaven that lies within, receives everything from there and He is incessantly established on the truth of His divine nature.

The reappearance of tempter

For the second time the tempter appears before Jesus: *Matthew 4:5-7 "Then the devil took him into the holy city. He set him on the pinnacle of the temple, and said to him, 'If you are the Son of God, throw yourself down, for it is written, 'He will put his angels in charge of you.' and, 'On their hands they will bear you up, so that you don't dash your foot against a stone.' Jesus said to him, 'Again, it is written, 'You shall not test the Lord, your God.'"* For one more time the Devil challenges Jesus trying to spread in His mind and heart the poison of doubt and of selfishness. Questioning the wisdom and perfection of God, the devil asks Jesus to test God and to have certain external proof of His existence. For those who lack in faith and trust their own limited mentality more than the vastness of God's wisdom such words of the Devil may sound even logical. But for a true worshiper, for a devotee who has submitted each personal opinion at the feet of the divine and who has burnt so-called rationalism in the fire of feverish trust and renunciation, such temptations are totally meaningless.

Jesus is so perfectly established on the realization of His true nature and so focused internally that He doesn't respond to such temptations. The Devil for the third time is tempting Jesus and tries to bend the straight and unwavering mast of His renunciation: *Matthew 4:8-10 "Again, the devil took him to an exceedingly high mountain, and showed him all the kingdoms of the world, and their glory. He said to him, 'I will give you all of these things, if you will fall down and worship me.' Then Jesus said to him, 'Get behind me, Satan! For it is written, 'You shall worship the Lord your God, and you shall serve him only.'"* The devil uses his last weapon to break the commitment of Jesus. Through greed he expects to attract Jesus' attention to him and challenges Him to obtain all the materialistic wealth. How many are those who actually obey this command of the devil and finally cooperate with him!

Jesus knows well that the gold of the eternal life close to His creator cannot be compared with the dirt of the temporary mundane wealth, thus He clearly explains that those who worship God cannot worship simultaneously Mammon, the deity of material wealth, and vice versa: *Luke 16:13 "No servant can serve two masters, for either he will hate the one, and love the other; or else he will hold to one, and despise the other. You aren't able to serve God and mammon.'"* The one pointed focus of Jesus swallows all the five snakes that the devil tries desperately to enter within His soul lust, greed, attachment, anger and egotism. Finally the Devil leaves and Jesus, charged with the strength of these harsh austerities, begins the wonderful and perfect route of His mission.

THE TEACHINGS OF JESUS CHRIST: THE SPIRITUAL PRINCIPLES THAT PAVE THE PATH TO THE CRUCIFIXION

The two commandments and their significance

A beautiful expression of Jesus' teaching can be found in the two basic commandments which we encounter in the Gospel of Mark spoken by Jesus Himself when He is asked which commandment is the most important of all: *Mark 12:29-31 "Jesus answered, 'The greatest is, 'Hear, Israel, the Lord our God, the Lord is one: you shall love the Lord your God with all your heart, and with all your soul, and with all your mind, and with all your strength.' This is the first commandment. The second is like this, 'You shall love your neighbor as yourself. There is no other commandment greater than these.'"* The message of oneness, of unconditional love for God and for all His creatures reflects the core of the teachings of Jesus. How significant it is to comprehend the sacred complement of these two commandments. Once the devotee realizes through his constant love for the divine that he is a part and parcel of Him, then he is able to love everyone as His creation and serve each one selflessly, seeing actually no separation, no distinction. Vice versa, when a devotee annihilates himself and his needs, when he crosses the marsh of egotism and the sense of 'mine' by loving others unconditionally with no sense of possession or attachment then, through this selfless love and service, all the mental and physical impurities can be removed and the revelation of his true divine nature can take place.

The deep pain for our separation from Him and the ardent longing of our soul, mind and heart for the reunion with Him signal the harmony to Jesus' first commandment. His second commandment defines perfectly the actual meaning of love, which is all about expanding our consciousness, going beyond the limitations of our physical body. When we love our neighbor as an inseparable part of our self, we dive into the ocean of compassion and self-sacrifice. Inside this vast ocean, the confinement of ego dissolves. Only this selfless love has the tremendous power to melt our harshness and liberate us from the clutches of ignorance, of identifying ourselves with this gross body.

Still, the obedience to these two commandments and their fulfillment is the gate to the kingdom of the teaching of Jesus: *Matthew 19:16-17 "Behold, one came to him and said, 'Good teacher, what good thing shall I do, that I may have eternal life?' He said to him, 'Why do you call me good? No one is good but one, that is, God. But if you want to enter into life, keep the commandments.'"* The eternal life signifies the true message of Jesus' teaching while following the commandments constitutes the straight path to this ultimate goal. Jesus teaches undoubtedly through His bright example the virtues of humility, forgiveness, self-annihilation, sacrifice for others, simplicity, renunciation, service and feverish love even for the enemies. Indeed all these virtues are the qualifications to dive into the ocean of His magnanimous message, which is eternal life, immortality, divine transformation. The actualization of His message can be accomplished through His descent in every aspirant who surrenders to the divine and experiences the supreme state of divine unity and eternal bliss.

The fulfillment and actualization of the commandments will make the winding roads straight, will make the rough paths smooth, will cleanse all the inner impurities so that the devotees will be ready to walk the path that Jesus has opened before them: *John 14:12 "Most certainly I tell you, he who believes in me, the works that I do, he will do also; and he will do greater works than these, because I am going to my Father."* With these perfect words, Jesus calls us to tread the divine path that is eternal and extraordinary. He reassures us that this evolutionary path will expand incessantly, thus the sincere devotees will perform even higher tasks than those, which we encounter in the Bible. Of course, we should always remember that all these supernatural powers and miracles, all these great works are not for the sake of amazement or attraction of the crowds. How such pitiful motivation could emanate from the magnanimous soul of Jesus! The actual motivation of these miracles, as we see through His example, is the torrent of supreme compassion towards every being. Each cell of His totality oozes this nectar of compassion and this causes the manifestation of such miraculous powers for the relief, the cure and the peace of all those who are suffering. They are meant to empower and inspire everyone to tread the path of ultimate truth following the reliable tracks of Jesus. It is not enough to merely appreciate and admire His teachings or accept His words intellectually without applying them into practice in our day-to-day life. Jesus clearly asks us to follow His tracks, stand on our feet and become His honorable successors. So tenderly, as a loving father, He is asking us to become the sons of His Resurrection, to reflect through our totality that we are His immortal children.

The virtues inside the ocean of Jesus' teaching

Undoubtedly the New Testament – through the Gospels and the Epistles of the Apostles – spreads, as a lighthouse, the bright rays of further understanding and elaboration of these virtues, which are significant for everyone who craves to dive into the vast ocean of Jesus' teachings. To sanctify the lake of the five poisons i.e. greed, lust, anger, attachment and egotism, we have to make a link with the fresh and clear water of this ocean and let this rushing water transform the lake into a pure reflection of ocean itself. The water is always the same, it is always a part and parcel of the Creator, yet the veil of ignorance has created the distinction between the lake and the ocean. All the virtues that are being taught by Jesus provide us with a life fully dedicated to the divine and establish this link in the root of our existence. This link connects the devotee with the source of eternal wisdom and compassion and ultimately the most basic sin, which is actually ignorance itself, is extinguished.

In fact, this ignorance about our true immortal nature is all that has to be rectified. And for those who have been set free from this sin—from which all the other impurities emanate—opens the gate to the essence of Jesus' message as Paul writes with such beauty and lucidness in his Epistle to *Romans 6:22-23 "But now, being made free from sin, and having become servants of God, you have your fruit of sanctification, and the result of eternal life. For the wages of sin is death, but the free gift of God is eternal life in Christ Jesus our Lord."* How lucidly Paul is explaining that the eternal life is in Jesus, in the awakening of our inherent divine potential under His eternal compassionate guidance. Nowadays, many scientists try through external sources to achieve the state of immortality, of eternal life. Still, all these researches are merely for the sake of longevity and not for the essential eternal life that constitutes the gist of Jesus' teachings. The eternal Kingdom of Heaven that lies within each one of us is the final destination and the passage to It is Jesus. The ultimate core of His teachings is the eternal life, the reflection of the Lord's glory through each iota of our existence and the medium to this supreme goal is to live according to His commands with feverish faith and one-pointed focus: *Philippians 3:20-21 "For our citizenship is in heaven, from where we also wait for a Savior, the Lord Jesus Christ; who will change the body of our humiliation to be conformed to the body of his glory, according to the working by which he is able even to subject all things to himself."*

Before approaching the pinnacle of Jesus' message for complete divinization of the human being at every level, it will be really enlightening to contemplate the virtues, which will provide the necessary fertile land for the divine manifestation and descent. The purification and peace of mind will remove all the impediments and prepare the appropriate ground for the gradual transformation of the physical body itself, which leads to the actual fulfillment of Jesus' teaching for immortal eternal life: *Romans 12:2 "Don't be conformed to this world, but be transformed by the renewing of your mind, so that you may prove what is the good, well-pleasing, and perfect will of God."*

Compassion: the foundation of Jesus' teachings

Compassion is the fundamental ground for the colonnade of all the virtues that Jesus is teaching. It nourishes the branches of unconditional love, selfless service, humbleness, forgiveness and kindness. Compassion, especially for those who have gone astray, constitutes the core of Jesus' teachings and is reflected in His behavior throughout His life. Jesus being an endless reservoir of inspiration, aspiration, strength and commitment to the divine will, calls us to break all the confinements of our ego and have supreme compassion for others. This is possible only when we become aware of our true origin, that we are His children. Only then, we are able to overcome the identification with our physical body and expand our consciousness to such an extent that we see and serve everyone as Him. The realization that everything is His manifestation, that nothing is separated from Him, that we are an inseparable part of Him and so is every other being is the actual foundation of compassion, which is the ultimate value and which supports all the rest spiritual virtues.

Matthew 10:39 "He who seeks his life will lose it; and he who loses his life for my sake will find it." How clearly Jesus is teaching us the path that leads towards the eternal life! Only by dissolving the ego in the fertile soil of compassion, the vast tree of our divine inherent nature can manifest and reveal its grandeur. Those who dissolve their ego in the soil of compassion and expand so widely their consciousness, feeling His presence everywhere can live eternally in Him. The crucifixion of ego and the unlimited compassion for others can wipe out all the physical and mental impurities. When the sense of separation from others is gone, then the self-sacrifice sprouts and we unite with everyone and everything around us, beyond any limitation. As the nature of the river is to flow, accepting the different streams from all the directions, and finally merge into the sea, similarly, a heart which is full of compassion flows harmoniously with everything that surrounds it. This compassionate heart welcomes everyone, without restriction, along its route and ultimately unites with God, the primordial source of everything in this universe: *John 3:3 "Jesus answered him, 'Most certainly, I tell you, unless one is born anew, he can't see the Kingdom of God.'"* The compassion is the most essential tool for the birth from above, since only through self annihilation and crucifixion of the sense of 'I' and 'mine' the actual renovation can take place inside us and lead us to the resurrection, to our ultimate predestination.

Unconditional love - forgiveness

The grand mountain of Jesus' teachings, well rooted in compassion, has an ultimate ridge formed from 2 slopes: unconditional love and forgiveness. This mountain crest rises with such divine nobility and celestial beauty and it is actually the cornice of this great mountain. Unconditional love is the side of the mountain leading upwards, since to be able to love everyone as an inseparable part of Him we have to uplift and expand our consciousness to extreme heights and breadths. Forgiveness is the side of the mountain that leads downwards since to forgive we have to bend our ego, bow before the divinity that dwells in everyone and dive into the sea of supreme compassion and understanding for others.

Matthew 5:44-48 "But I tell you, love your enemies, bless those who curse you, do good to those who hate you, and pray for those who mistreat you and persecute you, that you may be children of your Father who is in heaven. For he makes his sun to rise on the evil and the good, and sends rain on the just and the unjust. For if you love those who love you, what reward do you have? Don't even the tax collectors do the same? If you only greet your friends, what more do you do than others? Don't even the tax collectors do the same? Therefore you shall be perfect, just as your Father in heaven is perfect." Jesus calls us to remain in His love and overcome all the limitations that tend to separate us from others, that nourish the selfishness, the harshness and the discrimination. When we cannot love everyone without any restriction and limitation, in fact, we cannot relate with God as well, who is the ultimate source of eternal life. Thus, by not being able to see the divinity that resides in every single being we condemn ourselves to decay, to deterioration, to mortality. As long the water remains confined to a limited place and does not flow freely towards the sea, it is bound to eventually become a filthy marsh. Similarly, as long we confine ourselves to a so limited egoistic existence, we are bound to be spoiled and eventually perish.

John 13:34-35 "A new commandment I give to you, that you love one another, just like I have loved you; that you also love one another. By this everyone will know that you are my disciples, if you have love for one another." To love and serve everyone with the sincerity, unselfishness and grandness that Jesus is teaching us signals with uttermost clarity that we have become His disciples. Only then His teachings have actually penetrated the rock of our dry mentality and rationalism, they have pierced the knot of our rigid individuality and we become His children, full of innocence and purity: *John 15:9-10 "Even as the Father has loved me, I also have loved you. Remain in my love. If you keep my commandments, you will remain in my love; even as I have kept my Father's commandments, and remain in his love."* Jesus Christ, the veracious companion of our souls, so tenderly expresses His constant love for us through these words. He calls us to follow His example by loving God and each other so deeply and truly as He does for us. Each devotee who abides in the Lord's love experiences the supreme bliss and innermost peace of His endless and unlimited love.

In the first letter of John, a bouquet of wonderful verses, glorifying the fellowship with God through the perfect love for others, spreads a celestial fragrance. *1 John 3:14 "We know that we have passed out of death into life, because we love the brothers. He who doesn't love his brother remains in death."* Whoever loves is a child of God and knows God. Whoever loves God must love others also, since with the pure eyes of a child he realizes that everything originates, resides and exists in Him. Everyone, who remains united with the ultimate divine source, lives eternally. But when he is divided and disconnected from the source, is condemned to death. As the drop dissolves into the sea and becomes one with it, similarly when we merge into the ocean of the divine love our ego dissolves and we become essentially one with Him; we reestablish in our true immortal nature and gain the victory upon death.

Inwards focus

Jesus unceasingly asks from His disciples, through His parables and teachings, to merge into inwardness and turn their attention and concentration deeply within: *Luke 17:20-21 "Being asked by the Pharisees when the Kingdom of God would come, he answered them, 'The Kingdom of God doesn't come with observation; neither will they say, 'Look, here!' or, 'Look, there!' for behold, the Kingdom of God is within you.'"* The continuous introspection and reflection upon our true nature will sharpen our discrimination and hone our self-knowledge. Thus the tendency to focus on and judge other's faults and shortcomings will cease, since we will see clearly the darkness of the mental and physical impurities within us that need to be removed with the light of Jesus' teachings: *Matthew 23:11-12 "But he who is greatest among you will be your servant. Whoever exalts himself will be humbled, and whoever humbles himself will be exalted."*

This realization will prepare the appropriate ground of humbleness and service to others, since if we ourselves have not explored the source of divine light that resides within us, then how will we be able to spread this light around? *Luke 6:41-42 "Why do you see the speck of chaff that is in your brother's eye, but don't consider the beam that is in your own eye? Or how can you tell your brother, 'Brother, let me remove the speck of chaff that is in your eye,' when you yourself don't see the beam that is in your own eye? You hypocrite! First remove the beam from your own eye, and then you can see clearly to remove the speck of chaff that is in your brother's eye."* With a breathtaking lucidity, Jesus explains that there is no scope for judgment and criticism of others inside the heart of a sincere disciple who tries to cleanse himself internally and unite with God. Humbleness is the precious fruit of the inwards focus. Only by turning our focus inside, we will be able to realize where we actually stand, what are the impurities that pollute our thoughts, words and deeds. With humility and under the guidance of Lord, we can explore ourselves through deep introspection. This self-exploration will cease our tendency to expect others to change and we will rather consciously redirect our attention and concentration towards our own selves, where the actual change can take place: *Mark 7:15 "There is nothing from outside of the man, that going into him can defile him; but the things which proceed out of the man are those that defile the man."* Everything that connects us with the primordial inner source, the omniscient, omnipresent and omnipotent God is pious and sacred. On the contrary, whatever creates a disconnection to this source is actually sinful and profane. As long we remain inside our inherent divine kingdom, nothing can affect or threaten our peace and stillness. When we lose the connection with the divine, then piety is turned to evilness that is reflected in our actions-words and desecrates the holiness of our being.

Renunciation

The virtues that disciples cultivate within their hearts for inner and external restoration and transformation, lead to the crucifixion of all passions, desires and attachments. As long as the glamour of this external world attracts our eyes, we cannot have the clear vision of God. As long as we are entangled to this perishable, unreliable and temporary glitter of the outer word there is no scope for the eternal, true and everlasting glory of God. Therefore, renunciation is one of the major virtues on this path and many times we see clearly Jesus asking from His devotees to resist being slaves to anything external and turn to the Creator Himself, to the giver of eternal bliss: *Romans 1:24-25 "Therefore God also gave them up in the lusts of their hearts to uncleanness, that their bodies should be dishonored among themselves, who exchanged the truth of God for a lie, and worshiped and served the creature rather than the Creator, who is blessed forever. Amen."* The devotee, who has surrendered each of his breaths to the Lord and seeks nothing less than fusion and union with Him, is the one who worships the Creator. He yearns for the real life and the actual understanding of Jesus' message: *Colossians 3:2-4 "Set your mind on the things that are above, not on the things that are on the earth. For you died, and your life is hidden with Christ in God. When Christ, our life, is revealed, then you will also be revealed with him in glory."*

The precious eternal treasure is the glorious call of Jesus for the immortal life, for the total transformation by becoming a direct channel of divinity. This is our ultimate predestination and the common destiny that God has designed for all of us. The contentment with what we have already got and the cessation of the continuous hunt for further materialistic wealth, fame and name, for fulfillment of personal desires and attachments, bring peace in the mind and heart. They redirect the whole focus to God, to the true wealth: *1 Timothy 6:7 "For we brought nothing into the world, and we certainly can't carry anything out."* Jesus' message for innermost dispassion for any external possession, reveals clearly the divine property that resides within us and in fact shows how futile is our attachment to anything in this world. This exclusive and zealous devotion to God with the realization that we are all His children sprouts a vast sense of brotherhood with every being around us: *Matthew 12:48-50 "But he answered him who spoke to him, 'Who is my mother? Who are my brothers?'He stretched out his hand towards his disciples, and said, "Behold, my mother and my brothers! For whoever does the will of my Father who is in heaven, he is my brother, and sister, and mother.'"* By renouncing all the desires and attachments that take us away from the ultimate source of life and energy – the Almighty – and by rejecting everything that is false and delusionary, we unveil the truth that that He is the Father of all and therefore, everyone becomes naturally our sister and brother. Being linked with the Father, we understand that everything in this universe originates from Him and belongs to Him. We recognize Him as the ultimate reality, as the absolute truth and we renounce anything else, considering it meaningless and futile.

Burning childlike faith

Undoubtedly, one of the main teachings of Jesus' is the necessity of having a pure and innocent heart full of burning childlike faith. This is reflected clearly in the impressive simplicity of His words and parables, and in the absolute harmony among His words, thoughts and deeds. Being an innocent and truthful Son, He unfolds the divine will with unwavering faith and heartedly trust towards His Father: *John 18:20 "Jesus answered him, "I spoke openly to the world. I always taught in synagogues, and in the temple, where the Jews always meet. I said nothing in secret."* The flaming childlike faith burns all the fears, doubts or worries and provides us with such courage and power to face any obstacle on our path to God–realization. Therefore, virgin purity and heartiest trust of the child must be cultivated within the heart of every devotee: *1 Peter 2:2-3 "As newborn babies, long for the pure milk of the Word, that you may grow thereby, if indeed you have tasted that the Lord is gracious."* We should come and knock at the Lord's door with childlike joy and honesty and He will open His door at once: *Mark 11:24 "Therefore I tell you, all things whatever you pray and ask for, believe that you have received them, and you shall have them."* As the nightingale twitters before the dawn, in absolute darkness, welcoming the arrival of a new bright day, similarly, so strong and firm should be our faith. Even, when apparent adversities and difficulties dominate and cloud cover the light of hope and aspiration, we should always chant the Name of God having total faith in His enlightening compassion and love, which can totally dispel this darkness. By believing in His everlasting providence, our heart fills with unshaken and unquestioning faith and we experience the supreme bliss of His eternal companionship: *John 12:36 "While you have the light, believe in the light, that you may become children of light." Jesus said these things, and he departed and hid himself from them."*

With bright eyes turned inwards as those of an infant we will be able to face the Grandeur of Lord's Glory: *Luke 11:34 "The lamp of the body is the eye. Therefore when your eye is good, your whole body is also full of light; but when it is evil, your body also is full of darkness."* The healthy sight of the child who is always willing to explore with an open mind the secrets of divine creation, who is always ready to run to mother's lap and with peaceful mind relax in this shelter having no worry or doubt, is the one that every disciple should adopt through gradual inner purification and continuous practice. Admitting our need for the divine mother's protection and by having full trust in Her providence, we should walk on the spiritual path as small children: *Luke 11:9 "I tell you, keep asking, and it will be given you. Keep seeking, and you will find. Keep knocking, and it will be opened to you."* It is this childlike faith, which moves a woman to merely touch Jesus' cloak and immediately be cured from her disease. How indicative is the reply of Jesus to this woman: *Mark 5:34 "He said to her, 'Daughter, your faith has made you well. Go in peace, and be cured of your disease.'"*

To strengthen this pure innocent faith and determination to tread the path of God realization, Jesus performed numerous miracles, which emanate from the inexhaustible source of supreme compassion for all the creation. He serves the whole humanity in order to inspire it to enter into the Kingdom of God and relieves it from all the physical, mental and spiritual obstacles so that it will continue its route more charged, vivid and qualified. Hundreds are the cases where He cures, in miraculous ways, the diseases of people who approach Him. He is actually a direct link of God's energy and He even enables people to join with this flow and be part of it. In every single miracle of Jesus, which is mentioned in the Bible, we see the same goal, the empowerment of childlike faith in the hearts of the disciples. Miracles such as the healing of the paralyzed, blind and deaf people and of those who are possessed by evil spirits; the resurrection of dead people; the transfiguration of Jesus before the eyes of His disciples and His supernatural abilities to walk on the water, to cease the wind, to cure people with one of His mere touches; the miraculous feeding of thousand people with the minimum external nutrition; all of them aim to strengthen the faith. They empower the certainty that for those who live in Christ everything is possible and there is no limitation or bondage: *1 Corinthians 2:9 "But as it is written, 'Things which an eye didn't see, and an ear didn't hear, which didn't enter into the heart of man, these God has prepared for those who love him.'"*

The bliss of living in Christ

The passage to the gate of the Lord's message is the inner purification through these outstanding spiritual principles, which qualify the devotee to be in tune with the spirit of the Lord. With these values, the disciple is able and deserves to dive into the ocean of the essential message of Jesus, in the goal itself, into the core of His descent on this earth. True happiness belongs to those who live in Christ, to those who seek the eternal life, to those who are inspired to tread the path for God realization at any cost with all their heart, mind, might and soul. Inner purification brings enlightenment and enlightenment leads to perfection, to the descent of God at every level, to His dominance in every single part of our being.

The words of Jesus at the Sermon on the Mount include, with amazing clarity and extraordinary beauty, the true prosperity that lies within the one who has surrendered everything at the feet of God and constantly experiences the eternal bliss of self-realization, of self-knowledge, of complete surrender to God and selfless service to all His manifestations.

Matthew 5:1-12

"Seeing the multitudes, he went up onto the mountain. When he had sat down, his disciples came to him. He opened his mouth and taught them, saying,
'Blessed are the poor in spirit, for theirs is the Kingdom of Heaven.
Blessed are those who mourn, for they shall be comforted.
Blessed are the gentle, for they shall inherit the earth.
Blessed are those who hunger and thirst after righteousness, for they shall be filled.
Blessed are the merciful, for they shall obtain mercy.
Blessed are the pure in heart, for they shall see God.

Blessed are the peacemakers, for they shall be called children of God. Blessed are those who have been persecuted for righteousness' sake, for theirs is the Kingdom of Heaven.

Blessed are you when people reproach you, persecute you, and say all kinds of evil against you falsely, for my sake. Rejoice, and be exceedingly glad, for great is your reward in heaven. For that is how they persecuted the prophets who were before you.'"

UNFOLDING THE DIVINE WILL: THE CRUCIFIXION OF JESUS CHRIST

Through His teachings, Jesus spreads the message of transcendence from our false identification with the body, the mind, the senses, the limited individuality, to the actual realization that we are essentially divine. For almost three years Jesus teaches incessantly, accompanied by His twelve disciples and pours in the hearts of all who believe in Him the divine fuel of understanding the depth of His words and the core of His mission. Numerous teachings – through parables, plentiful miracles and abundant inner experiences of those who are granted to surround Him and follow His commands – set the path for the final crucifixion of every physical, spiritual and mental limitation and bondage.

The fulfillment of the Divine Plan

As for a tree when its root is diseased, all the branches and leaves become ill, similarly, the original sin of Adam and Eve – who constitute the root of human race – has condemned us to corruption, to mortality. However, the compassionate Almighty, moved from His immense love for all His children, has planned the restoration to our primary celestial state as it was before the fall and the transgression of Adam and Eve. The rectification of the original sin, of our disconnection and estrangement from our Heavenly Father, comes through His Son, Jesus Christ, who takes flesh and blood and incarnates the Logos.

Jesus is the vehicle of the divinity up to earth and paves, through His teachings and life, the path that leads us to the reunion with our inherent immortal nature. He, the *Theanthropos*, being a perfect God and a perfect man, is the Savior of the humankind, deifying the human nature through His Resurrection. He provides to everyone the opportunity to reach to *theosis*, to attain divinity. Every happening in Jesus' life reflects clearly how God has designed everything so perfectly and how all the appropriate circumstances have been set for the fulfillment of the divine plan. Jesus follows with absolute faith the commands of God and every action of Him serves to reveal God's will. Exhibiting absolute surrender to the divine arrangements, He is flowing harmoniously with every part of this plan and accepting everything, glorious or humiliating, with no resistance.

After three years of feverish teachings to the masses and preparing His disciples to follow the divine path, He realizes that the necessary ground has been set and the time is ripe for the crescendo of His mission on earth through His Resurrection. He is fully aware that the deification of the human nature cannot be accomplished without the demolishment of the ego. Since body is the abidance of ego, causing our separation from others and the divine, it has to vanish, to die. The death of all the physical limitations and the crucifixion of ego will ultimately lead to the manifestation of our divine nature. Jesus knows that His victory upon the ultimate enemy, the death, is the only way to resurrection. However, this victory is not possible without the divine descent unto the grossest form, the physical body. Jesus, by becoming a concrete example of divinization at every level, even the physical, opens the gate to all those who aspire to tread the path and motivates them to keep on evolving incessantly. So that, by knowing the ultimate destination through His example, sincere seekers will not be fooled, misguided or go astray misinterpreting the milestones for the goal.

Jesus, the Holy Son, invokes His Divine Father to manifest His glory through the channel of His physical body, since it is only the Divine Grace that can divinize this perishable nature of the body; that can lead it from Adam's mortality to Jesus' immortality: *John 17:4-5 "I glorified you on the earth. I have accomplished the work which you have given me to do. Now, Father, glorify me with your own self with the glory which I had with you before the world existed."* Life in this physical world is overpowered by death. Still, the ultimate power belongs to the omnipotent God, the overflowing source of eternal life. Only His Grace can swallow the death and transform its venomous poison to nectar of immortality: *1 Corinthians 15:53-54 "For this corruptible must put on incorruption, and this mortal must put on immortality. But when this corruptible will have put on incorruption, and this mortal will have put on immortality, then what is written will happen: "Death is swallowed up in victory."*

As a seed does not sprout to life unless it dissolves in soil; as wood does not produce fire unless it is burnt; similarly, the perishable body has to die to become imperishable. All the limitations of the mortal body have to be pierced, so that immortality can be accomplished. Jesus with His Resurrection, sets the example before our eyes, by crossing through the darkness of the uttermost Hades and returning back to life being physically transformed, attaining an immortal body. However, it is only through the rays of the Divine Grace that this darkness can be dispelled; therefore, Jesus is very particular to invocate the grace of His Heavenly Father for this grand accomplishment.

Obviously, Adam and Eve are expelled from the Garden of Eden not to be doomed but to return back to it, fully conscious and illumined, reflecting the glory of their divine heritage. The Heavenly Father exiles His children from His kingdom to provide them the opportunity to grow, explore and manifest their complete divine potential, much like the mother bird that forces out its reluctant young chick so that it can learn to fly.

The Lord's Supper

Jesus Christ, the tender Shepherd, caring so deeply for the salvation of His flock sacrifices Himself through His Crucifixion that eventually leads to His Resurrection. As the divine plan approaches its peak, He signals all the forthcoming events, giving to His disciples certain indications about them. He is so considerate for His apostles, who are playing, unknowingly, a crucial role in the divine arrangements, while He is completely conscious of His unique mission. Out of compassion, He foretells these events, so that they will not be worried, fearful or upset when the climax of the divine plan will take place. Being informed about these events, they will have no doubt that they are true and they will be fully prepared to encounter the miraculous enactment of the divine plan. They will realize that their Master is the Son of God, the Holiest of all: *John 14:29 "Now I have told you before it happens so that, when it happens, you may believe."*

Unfolding the divine plan, Jesus gathers His disciples into a supper on the first day of the Jewish festival of Unleavened Bread. This is known as Lord's Supper, and Jesus informs them about His betrayal by one of them, which will lead to His arrest and eventually to His crucifixion. *Mark 14:18 "As they sat and were eating, Jesus said, 'Most certainly I tell you, one of you will betray me—he who eats with me.'"* Jesus, firmly established on His true origin, on His divine nature, acts with the most idealistic way knowing in advance that one of His disciples will betray Him. He is fully aware that this role will be given to Judas, who decides to betray His Master. For thirty silver coins as a reward, Judas cooperates with the Jewish authorities who accuse Him that He has committed a crime claiming that He is the King of Jews. However, Lord is not resisting the divine plan, but being absolutely still and peaceful, as a loyal servant of God, He surrenders unconditionally to the divine will. His behavior sketches with the most splendid colors the ideal state of a true servant who has applied his logic, mind, body and every belonging to God's will and is a deserving carrier of divine grace. How rare, in this cosmos, are such sincere servants, who dissolve their existence in the fertile land of their Master and develop spiritually, as the seed flourishes only when it is absorbed in soil.

Each incidence, in the Lord's Supper, is truly enlightening and carries a special significance, reflecting the wisdom of the divine plan and the magnanimous compassion of Lord. Initially, Jesus washes His disciple's feet, pointing that there is one amongst them who is not clean, meaning Judas, who is planning to betray Him few hours after the supper. With innermost humility and equanimity, Jesus sets before them a flawless example of a sincere servant: *John 13:14-16 "I then, the Lord and the Teacher, have washed your feet, you also ought to wash one another's feet. For I have given you an example, that you also should do as I have done to you. Most certainly I tell you, a servant is not greater than his lord, neither one who is sent greater than he who sent him."* Jesus, protects His children, through these words, from the venomous poison of arrogance and pride. Those who tread the divine path, must be so humble as He is and should not carry, at all, any sense of superiority amongst each other or towards their master. Humility is the precious fruit of wisdom and the foundation for purity and serenity.

Jesus, having the perfect knowledge of everything, is a beau ideal for a Teacher. Generally, those who wish to become teachers educate themselves and eventually share with others all the knowledge they have gathered. Instead, for Jesus there is no need of such education since He is a born Teacher. His teachings are self-illumined and emanate directly from His communion with the fountain of wisdom, the omniscient God. With a breathtaking stoicism and understanding of the limits of human nature, Jesus accepts and respects its present situation. However, fully aware of His mission to deify this nature and elevate it to the highest divine realms, He embraces the humankind with such compassion and love. He is totally conscious that only through His Resurrection, the divinization of human nature can take place. Therefore, He is guiding all of us with such patience and concern, so that we, His immortal children, gradually will manifest our inherent divine nature and return consciously to the Kingdom of Heaven, where we belong.

According to the divine plan, crucifixion is the passage to resurrection, thus, Jesus exhorts Judas to do quickly what he is supposed to do so that the plan will be unfolded: *John 13:27 "[…] Then Jesus said to him, 'What you do, do quickly.'"* He is remaining fearless, doubtless and firm, knowing perfectly that His self-sacrifice is inevitable for the salvation of His children. After the departure of Judas, Jesus turns to the rest of His disciples and gives them the new commandment: *John 13: 33-35 "Little children, I will be with you a little while longer. You will seek me, and as I said to the Jews, 'Where I am going, you can't come,' so now I tell you. A new commandment I give to you, that you love one another, just like I have loved you; that you also love one another. By this everyone will know that you are my disciples, if you have love for one another."* At this juncture, Jesus informs His disciples about His ultimate destination towards His Father and prepares them for His forthcoming absence. He knows that the time is ripe for the swan song of the divine plan, through His Resurrection, and gives certain indications of what is going to happen. Also, He informs them about their present inability to join Him on this divine limitless route. They have not still broken the shells that limit their consciousness and condemn them to physical confinements. Therefore, out of His immense compassion, He gives a new commandment that will enable them, ultimately, to join Him.

He asks of His children to love each other in the same manner He loves them. He knows that only through love, they will be able to expand their consciousness and arise from the bodily bindings. This expansion will cultivate inside them all the necessary qualifications to tread the path of divine descent in every realm, even the gross one. By loving each other, they will crush all the confinements that block presently the way towards divinization, towards immortality. They have to start from the level they stand and purify initially their mentality through selfless love and self-sacrifice. This mental purity is the prerequisite for the physical purification and transformation. Love's power exterminates all the knots that ego creates and enables us to go beyond our individuality. Just as a river unites the streams from different directions, similarly, love connects everyone and everything beyond restriction. Recognizing the universal consciousness, the all-pervading Almighty, that is lying in every form, we elevate gradually our consciousness to higher realms and set the ground for the next step, the physical transformation.

Undoubtedly, the ever flowing Divine Grace is blowing eternally and supports, with tremendous compassion, the efforts of all His children. As long as we unfurl our sails and trust with full heart our Father, we can receive the breeze of His Grace and continue successfully our divine route. How beautifully Jesus expresses His deep compassion, ascertaining His disciples that He will appear again before their eyes, after His Resurrection, and will guide them on the path of God-realization. He is opening the way to all of us, paving the path with such attention and concern, excluding none from this evolutionary journey. Our ultimate predestination is the divinity and Jesus, the most reliable compass, is leading towards it: *John 14:2-4 "In my Father's house are many homes. If it weren't so, I would have told you. I am going to prepare a place for you. If I go and prepare a place for you, I will come again, and will receive you to myself; that where I am, you may be there also. Where I go, you know, and you know the way."*

All those who tread the path of Christ will enter this divine kingdom and be qualified to experience for themselves the essence of His teachings, the divine immortalization: *Luke 22:28-30 "But you are those who have continued with me in my trials. I confer on you a kingdom, even as my Father conferred on me, that you may eat and drink at my table in my Kingdom. You will sit on thrones, judging the twelve tribes of Israel."* During Lord's Supper, Jesus reveals to them that He will not drink again this wine until the day He drinks the new wine with them in His Father's Kingdom. The divine nectar, the ambrosia, oozing from the total union with God's consciousness, shall be from now on His only nutrition. By this, He indicates the overcoming of all the physical limitations, the devastation of the clutches of death, disease and decay. It signals the new state where all the gross elements will be divinely transformed. Jesus is ready to experience, through His Crucifixion, the absolute metamorphosis and the birth of a new immortal body reflective of the divine glory in each part of it. He asks His disciples to take part in the holy communion of divine transfiguration by absorbing the bread and wine that carry the essence of His body and blood, which is actually the divine light: *Matthew 26:26-28 "As they were eating, Jesus took bread, gave thanks for it, and broke it. He gave to the disciples, and said, 'Take, eat; this is my body.' He took the cup, gave thanks, and gave to them, saying, 'All of you drink it, for this is my blood of the new covenant, which is poured out for many for the remission of sins.'"*

How beautifully Jesus expresses His blessings to all His disciples, connecting them with each part of Him. His totality is overfilled by the Divine Grace to such an extent that the nectar of holiness oozes naturally. Whatever comes in contact with it, receives this divine nectar, becomes sanctified. As the ember is taken from the fire and placed on the dormant coals, lights them up, similarly, whoever takes part in such holy communion, receives the fire of His divinity, becomes one with His everlasting Light for now and ever and to the ages of the ages.

The prayer of Jesus on the Mount of Olives

After the completion of the Lord's Supper, Jesus goes with His disciples on the Mount of Olives, where He prays fervently to God: *Matthew 26:39 "He went forward a little, fell on his face, and prayed, saying, 'My Father, if it is possible, let this cup pass away from me; nevertheless, not what I desire, but what you desire.'"* Jesus, the perfect servant of God's will, communicates with His Father with great devotion and piety. He is a tool in His hands, a chariot of His will, a vehicle of His Grace. He neglects totally His individuality and personal will. He prays with so great craving for the fulfillment of the divine plan that His heart melts by the fire of this longing. From all the pores of His body comes the sweat of His feverish prayer, like drops of blood, and it is poured on the ground of the whole humanity. As sweat balances the internal heat of the body with the external temperature, similarly, Jesus' sweat balances the furnace of His compassionate heart with the global atmosphere around Him that is full of corruption and harshness.

This sweat, like *'drops of blood,'* signals the ultimate sacrifice of Jesus for the restoration to our primordial divine state. Jesus, the Messiah, charged with the Holy Spirit offers Himself for the evolution of the humankind and spreads, through His being, the celestial fragrance of the compassion. Generally, sweat carries the toxins of the body, its waste. But Jesus' body being totally virgin and self-illumined, till the deepest levels of it, carries no such impurities. His sweat, as blood, comes directly from His magnanimous heart and extends the life in the universe.

Prior to His prayer, Jesus has asked His disciples to remain alert and conscious, without falling to the clutches of slumber: *Matthew 26:40-41 "He came to the disciples, and found them sleeping, and said to Peter, 'What, couldn't you watch with me for one hour? Watch and pray, that you don't enter into temptation. The spirit indeed is willing, but the flesh is weak."* At this point, Jesus clearly understands how difficult for the humankind is to become a carrier of the divine descent at the gross level. As a pot will break into pieces if it is placed under a waterfall, being unable to hold its tremendous flow, similarly, the human body, in its present state, is so weak to hold the grandeur of the Holy Spirit, the vastness of the divine current. How mischievous the game of the senses is and how feeble the physical body is to receive the divine power. The disciples, entangled in the nets of slumber, cannot remain alert and conscious. Due to their extroverted focus and spiritual immaturity, the darkness of ignorance is still predominant inside them. They are not able to hold the divine light, overpowered by the mesmerizing sounds of Morpheus, by the alluring lullabies of this external world.

Thus, they disobey their Master's command, unintentionally. Jesus prays three times for them on the Mount of Olives before being arrested and watches clearly how strong the identification of His disciples with their physical body is. This illusionary identification doesn't allow them to follow Jesus on the path to ultimate restoration. Therefore, all His disciples betray Him and claim that they have no relation with Him, as He had already predicted: *John 16:32 "Behold, the time is coming, yes, and has now come, that you will be scattered, everyone to his own place, and you will leave me alone. Yet I am not alone, because the Father is with me."*

The narrow gate

As the peak of the divine plan approaches, Jesus remains alone and drinks the nectar of the divine companionship. None of His disciples can stand next to Him, being afraid and worried for their life. They deny their Master, since they still cannot cross the narrow gate that leads directly to the Kingdom of Heaven. As long as someone is carrying the load of worldly bearings and is attached to his physicality, he cannot pass through this gate. Only one who is fully naked of all the layers before God and crushes the limitations of his ego is qualified to cross it. The expanse of our worldly attractions and attachments cannot fit in such narrowness. To get through this gate we certainly need the compassionate guidance of a competent Master to help us unload. Jesus is the Shepherd, who is meant to lead all His children who keep a pure heart and yearn to enter this gate, surrendering to His commandments: *John 10:2-3 "But one who enters in by the door is the shepherd of the sheep. The gatekeeper opens the gate for him, and the sheep listen to his voice. He calls his own sheep by name, and leads them out."* The aspirants, who crave for nothing else than God and submit their life to Him; who do not wander in the jungles of these worldly attractions rather keep one-pointed focus on the goal and constant concentration; those aspirants will accomplish to stand at the narrow gate. Reaching there, they will be able to hear clearly the calling of the divine Shepherd and follow Him at once, with no hesitation.

As long our senses are focused outwards and the lure of this world attracts and carries away our attention, we disconnect from the divine source and go astray. But those who have exclusive love for God and rein the deer of desire from frisking around in the desert of sensual enjoyments, they can relate to the crystal-clear message of Jesus: *Matthew 7:13-14 "Enter in by the narrow gate; for wide is the gate and broad is the way that leads to destruction, and many are those who enter in by it. How narrow is the gate, and restricted is the way that leads to life! Few are those who find it."* Indeed how few are those who are granted to discover the narrow gate! Reaching there, they should keenly knock and seek the response from God. Praying for knowledge, discrimination, devotion and renunciation, they should knock with maximum and innermost sincerity and zeal. God is always there to embrace His children, yet the aspirants should make the leap, get inspired to knock the door and go beyond the limitations. Through the narrow gate of feverish service and practice, they will deserve the divine response: *Matthew 7:7-8 "Ask, and it will be given you. Seek, and you will find. Knock, and it will be opened for you. For everyone who asks receives. He who seeks finds. To him who knocks it will be opened."*

The arrest of Jesus Christ

In accordance with the perfectly designed divine plan, Jesus Christ is arrested by the Roman soldiers since Judas informs them where He is. Jesus is sent before Pilate by the Jewish authorities with the accusation that He has committed a crime claiming that He is the King of Jews. Pilate asks Jesus if He is the King and from His answers he cannot find any reason to condemn Him. Nevertheless, he sentences Jesus to death at the urging of the chief priests as they feel insulted and threatened due to the power of His true words. These revealing truths expose their hypocrisy and misinterpretation of the Holy Scriptures and the Divine Laws: *John 18:37-38 "Pilate therefore said to him, 'Are you a king then?' Jesus answered, 'You say that I am a king. For this reason I have been born, and for this reason I have come into the world, that I should testify to the truth. Everyone who is of the truth listens to my voice.' Pilate said to him, 'What is truth?' When he had said this, he went out again to the Jews, and said to them, 'I find no basis for a charge against him.'* In the Gospel of John we find that Jesus remains totally silent to this question, showing that the truth is meant only for those who deserve to listen to it.

During all the years of His life, Jesus has been teaching unceasingly the truth to all those who are seeking sincerely for it. However, one should be worthy and innocent in his heart to receive the precious gift of truth. It cannot be received by a corrupted mind, full of greed, lust and envy, since in such filthy and limited ground there is no scope for the glory and vastness of truth. Pilate, for the sake of his protection and benefit, obeys the demands of the Jewish authorities and condemns Jesus to death, although he finds nothing to accuse Him for. He turns his back to his personal responsibility to serve and obey the truth. Out of the fear of going against the will of the chief priests and facing adversities, which could threaten his worldly power and prestige, he is not qualified to connect with the ever flowing fountain of truth, in the form of Jesus. Therefore, when he asks Jesus what truth is, he receives His silence.

Jesus knowing the hypocrisy of Pilate's heart deprives him from the unique opportunity to be linked with the truth through Him: *Matthew 7:6 "Don't give that which is holy to the dogs, neither throw your pearls before the pigs, lest perhaps they trample them under their feet, and turn and tear you to pieces."* Still, Jesus does not respond, feeling no fear or obligation towards the authorities. He is only obligated towards the authority of the truth and manifests it before those eyes, which carry innocent faith and pious approach. Serving exclusively the Creator, Jesus reveals the truth only to those deserving candidates who are ready to accept its grandeur, unconditionally and at any cost. Undoubtedly, truth is inexplicable since it is not a matter to be approached mentally, but to live it. However, its principals can be perceived only from those who seek longingly for it and are willing to sacrifice everything in order to realize and actualize it. Therefore, Jesus knowing that heart of Pilate is dry from this longing prefers to keep silent.

The beginning of Jesus' final transformation

Jesus is sentenced to death and the beginning of His final transformation takes place, with this decision of the major authorities: *Mark 15:17-20 "They clothed him with purple, and weaving a crown of thorns, they put it on him. They began to salute him, 'Hail, King of the Jews!' They struck his head with a reed, and spat on him, and bowing their knees, did homage to him. When they had mocked him, they took the purple off of him, and put his own garments on him. They led him out to crucify him."* Jesus with immeasurable stoicism and innermost piety faces all this humiliation knowing that the root of this is ignorance. He accepts everything so peacefully, knowing perfectly what is yet to come. The perishable body is bound to die, since all its limitations have to be crushed. Still, death is not the final destination but an inevitable milestone on the grand path of divinization. The evolution of human nature is impossible without the collapse of these physical confinements, without death. Adam's heritage is corruption and mortality rooted in the original sin. Jesus' heritage is compassion and eternal life. Through His Resurrection, Jesus, the new Adam, will liberate the humankind from the original sin and will reappear for a second time to take along all His children who have a burning craving to unite with Him: *Hebrews 9:27-28 "Inasmuch as it is appointed for men to die once, and after this, judgment, so Christ also, having been offered once to bear the sins of many, will appear a second time, without sin, to those who are eagerly waiting for him for salvation."*

Jesus has merged His totality into the ocean of ultimate compassion and mercy, and with unquestioning faith and total devotion He accepts the divine will. He has already foretold His closest disciples all that which is taking place now: *Matthew 20:18-19 "Behold, we are going up to Jerusalem, and the Son of Man will be delivered to the chief priests and scribes, and they will condemn him to death, and will hand him over to the Gentiles to mock, to scourge, and to crucify; and the third day he will be raised up."* The crucifixion is an inevitable part of the resurrection: *Matthew 13:31-32 "He set another parable before them, saying, 'The Kingdom of Heaven is like a grain of mustard seed, which a man took, and sowed in his field; which indeed is smaller than all seeds. But when it is grown, it is greater than the herbs, and becomes a tree, so that the birds."* Jesus understands that the time has finally come to expand the small seed of individuality and grossness of the physical body to such an extent that all the limitations will break and every single being will be affected from this expansion.

The earthly body is ready to give its place to the heavenly one, according to the divine plan and Jesus is the One who will accomplish this state of supreme consciousness and transfiguration. The union with Adam till now led to mortality, from now on the union with Christ will lead to immortality: *1 Corinthians 15:45-47 "So also it is written, 'The first man, Adam, became a living soul.' The last Adam became a life-giving spirit. However, that which is spiritual isn't first, but that which is natural, then that which is spiritual. The first man is of the earth, made of dust. The second man is the Lord from heaven."*

Victory upon death- Mission Immortality

It is really crucial to note again, at this point, that when Jesus speaks about the eternal life and the victory over the last enemy, death, He doesn't speak allegorically or symbolically about overcoming merely the fear of death. Literally, He speaks about the death of all physical, mental, intellectual and spiritual limitations and impurities which block the way for the complete manifestation of the divine. Jesus has given a foretaste of this celestial manifestation to His three disciples – Peter, John and James – through His transfiguration to divine light, at the mount Tabor: *Matthew 17:2-3 "He was transfigured before them. His face shone like the sun, and his garments became as white as the light. Behold, Moses and Elijah appeared to them talking with him."* In this miraculous incident of transfiguration, the three holy personalities – Jesus, Moses and Elijah – guiding all those who crave to tread the path of mission immortality, have exhibited the absolute freedom in themselves. Through their transformed body, purified mind and sanctified intellect they have been carriers of the divine descent. They have accomplished total freedom from all the external means, by spending long periods of isolation, fasting, disconnection from the outer world and total submission to the divine will. The three of them are the channels of the divine will and guide all those who aspire to walk on the immortal path with one-pointed focus and exclusive love for the divine.

The transfiguration of Jesus on the mount Tabor serves as a prelude to all that, which is yet to happen. Jesus, through His Resurrection, will transfigure to a divine immortal body and ultimately reappear before the eyes of all His servants. He will be accessible to all those who succeed, by His Grace, in knocking when the time is ripe and eventually enter into the ocean of God realization. Peter, John and James can connect with Moses and Elijah, because they are totally devoted to Jesus Christ who is the direct link with the enlightened divine Shepherds of all the ages and opens the gate for all His children.

During that incident of transfiguration, Peter asks Jesus to remain on the mountain and enjoy for ever this divine company of Him, Moses and Elijah. How great is the reply of the magnanimous Father: *Matthew 17:5 "While he was still speaking, behold, a bright cloud overshadowed them. Behold, a voice came out of the cloud, saying, 'This is my beloved Son, in whom I am well pleased. Listen to him.'"* The Heavenly Father ascertains the disciples that Jesus is His beloved Son, the chariot of His will on earth. He is well pleased with His Son's total surrendering to His commands. Similarly, they should obey with maximum discipline their Master's commands and apply their mind to Him. Jesus pacifies them telling them to not be afraid. Knowing that the peak of His mission will take place only through His Resurrection, before the eyes of all the sincere seekers of truth, He asks them to leave from the mountain.

At this juncture, the new command of Jesus is indicative of the grandeur of His mission on earth: *Matthew 17:9 "As they were coming down from the mountain, Jesus commanded them, saying, 'Don't tell anyone what you saw, until the Son of Man has risen from the dead.'"* This mission is not an individual matter concerning a few people but It expands universally and It includes everything in fact. Jesus' mission has such unlimited broadness and vastness, immeasurable depth and height, that all beings are affected by the light of His divine state, consciously or unconsciously. Jesus has clearly set the path that leads to purification, enlightenment and ultimately *theosis*. We are made according to God's image, thus, we have the latent potential to achieve this holy triptych. All we need to develop is sincere yearning to tread the unlimited evolutionary path, the path of Mission Immortality: *John 14:12 "Most certainly I tell you, he who believes in me, the works that I do, he will do also; and he will do greater works than these, because I am going to my Father."*

Jesus on the Cross

Jesus has already foretold the people that all those who are willing to sacrifice their individuality, they will be able to follow Him. Those who are ready to expand their consciousness and go beyond their physical limitations, they will be granted the eternal life. Those who remain confined to themselves they will condemned to mortality: *Mark 8:34-36 "He called the multitude to himself with his disciples, and said to them, 'Whoever wants to come after me, let him deny himself, and take up his cross, and follow me. For whoever wants to save his life will lose it; and whoever will lose his life for my sake and the sake of the Good News will save it. For what does it profit a man, to gain the whole world, and forfeit his life?"* Therefore, Jesus, all alone on His cross, is standing for the humankind and is ready to cross the threshold of Hades and return back to people in resurrected form.

Being sentenced to crucifixion, Jesus passes through gradual stages which reveal the divine plan more clearly. On the cross He refuses to drink the wine that is offered to Him by the soldiers. He craves to receive only the nectar which is already oozing from the inner source. At this moment of crucifixion, Jesus disconnects completely from this outer world and everything inside Him is lifted to the higher divine realms. His feet are not touching anymore this earth, this futile and limited external world does not matter to Him anymore. His total focus is on the absolute union with His Heavenly Father for the salvation of all His children. Being totally focused inwards, Jesus wishes to receive everything exclusively from the hands His Father. Therefore, he does not want to disturb the inner flow of the divine nectar by having anything external. He doesn't belong to the world anymore and He experiences at every subtle part of Himself the process of inner metamorphosis: *John 17:10-11 "All things that are mine are yours, and yours are mine, and I am glorified in them. I am no more in the world, but these are in the world, and I am coming to you. Holy Father, keep them through your name which you have given me, that they may be one, even as we are."*

The crescendo of ultimate compassion for all those who are ignorant is expressed by His words, which we meet in the Gospel of Luke when He is facing all the humiliation and mistreatment from the people who surround Him and who don't believe in His teachings: *Luke 23:34 "Jesus said, "Father, forgive them, for they don't know what they are doing. [...]"* As a kind and loving mother attends, with such sincere tenderness, to her child especially when it is in pitiful situation and badly needs her care, similarly, Jesus embraces all His children, especially the most ignorant ones. No one can be excluded from His vast lap, let that be His disciples, servants or even enemies and betrayers. As a shepherd cares mostly for his lost sheep, similarly Jesus longs especially to find all His lost children who have gone astray and are entangled inside the nets of ignorance. Having surrendered everything to the divine, Jesus expresses in a breathtaking way the vastness of His guiding compassion. Unceasingly He is fulfilling His mission and teaches the grandeur of forgiveness and selfless service to all, with no distinction or separation. The message of non duality finds its best expression in this statement and the glory of the universal oneness lightens the whole scene.

Jesus spreads His immense love to everyone who surrounds Him and treats each one with a unique understanding in order to evolve further: *John 19:25-27 "But there were standing by the cross of Jesus his mother, and his mother's sister, Mary the wife of Clopas, and Mary Magdalene. Therefore when Jesus saw his mother, and the disciple whom he loved standing there, he said to his mother, 'Woman, behold your son!' Then he said to the disciple, 'Behold, your mother!' From that hour, the disciple took her to his own home."* Jesus, feeling the extreme pain that burns the heart of All-Holy Mother Mary, pacifies Her with these so honest and tender words. He ascertains Her that from now on He will be close to Her in the form of His disciples to whom He has passed His spirit, His essential presence. Correspondingly, Jesus has deep concern for His beloved disciples. All-Holy Mother Mary, being in total union and harmony with the divine Son, will be from now on the sacred mother of all His servants, for all those who are related to Him and follow His path.

On His right and left two criminals are also sentenced to death: *Luke 23:39-43 "One of the criminals who was hanged insulted him, saying, "If you are the Christ, save yourself and us!" But the other answered, and rebuking him said, 'Don't you even fear God, seeing you are under the same condemnation? And we indeed justly, for we receive the due reward for our deeds, but this man has done nothing wrong.' He said to Jesus, 'Lord, remember me when you come into your Kingdom.' Jesus said to*

him, 'Assuredly I tell you, today you will be with me in Paradise.'"
How great is the message of this incident! Even at the ultimate moment of death, His grace is there ready to embrace and guide us to travel within to God's realization and communion. The moment we surrender to Him, that very moment all our impurities are sanctified and we belong to Him. Even at the last point, when vital divine energy is ready to depart from the physical body, we have the chance to connect with the Lord and realize that we are actually a part and parcel of Him. What is required is to turn our focus inwards, God wards, and apply everything to His will. The merciful Lord is always ready to take us into His lap and the gate to His Kingdom is always open wide every time, under any circumstance. We have to remove all the scales from our eyes and allow the divine energy to penetrate our individuality and to conquer each iota of our being.

The agony of separation

Gradually the process of inner transformation evolves at even deeper levels: *Mark 15:33-34 "When the sixth hour had come, there was darkness over the whole land until the ninth hour. At the ninth hour Jesus cried with a loud voice, saying, 'Eloi, Eloi, lama sabachthani?' which is, being interpreted, 'My God, my God, why have you forsaken me'"* The whole nature reflects the internal condition of Jesus Christ and the darkness foretells the coming of the supreme light through His perfect unity with God. Jesus, during all His life, has been feeling the celestial companionship of the Almighty, of His Heavenly Father. Approaching the peak of the divine plan – when His human nature will be merged into the divine and being deified and immortalized – He experiences for a moment a burning sense of separation from Him. God has always been next to

Him, descending in the form of Holy Spirit and guiding Him unceasingly. However, the time has come now for Jesus to take the leap and ascend to His Father. Before His final immersion to the divine, before merging His individuality to universal consciousness, He feels a great void.

This devout sense of separation causes severe agony, which intensifies His burning urge of reunion with God. This fire of urge burns all the gross elements of His physical form and the transformation of His physical body to a heavenly body begins. As gold enters into the fire and its burning adds to its glory and brightness, similarly, Jesus' physicality is burnt by the fire of this supreme longing and this adds to its illumination that ultimately leads to its divinization. The fire burns the grossness of earth and water in His body, refines them and transforms them to their subtlest form. All the senses have already turned inside and hence the vital energy of air rushes inwards with tremendous power and vividness, invigorating the flames of this fire that burn each part and inch of grossness in Jesus' body.

The flames of this immense craving cause inside Him the blazing sense of thirst. However, this thirst is not worldly so that it can be quenched by simple water or wine. It's only the divine nectar that can quench this thirst and Jesus seeks for it, with all His heart and might: *John 19:28-30 "After this, Jesus, seeing that all things were now finished, that the Scripture might be fulfilled, said, 'I am thirsty.' Now a vessel full of vinegar was set there; so they put a sponge full of the vinegar on hyssop, and held it at his mouth. When Jesus therefore had received the vinegar, he said, 'It is finished.' "He bowed his head, and gave up his spirit."* Jesus' task is complete, by taking the leap towards His Father. He has put all His efforts and now it is the time for the divine descent. Bowing His head, He surrenders completely to the Almighty and give up His spirit to the Creator.

The loud cry of Jesus

Jesus crosses the narrow gate with His unlimited devotional love for God and His absolute surrender. The flaming agony of separation from His Master prepares the fertile ground for the divine descent with the storm of devotional feelings. These feelings emanate straight from the heart of the most loyal devotee of God, from Jesus Christ. The agony of separation cleanses all the inner channels, the physical limitations and all are set for the manifestation of the divinity.

Jesus gives a loud cry and breathes His last. This loud cry penetrates and purifies all the physical blocks so that the nectar can flow throughout the body. It transforms all the gross elements and spreads the divine consciousness to each single cell siphoning thus the divine light and dispersing it to innumerable destinations. The loud cry – which actually emanates from the ultimate compassion and the complete surrendering to the divine will – clearly signifies the revocation of any blockage, obstruction or hindrance for the natural flow of ambrosia inside the immortalized body of Jesus Christ. The throat opens widely internally and all the knots are pierced, knots that could prevent the current of the divine nectar from the higher realms of the mind till the lowest parts of the body. As the first-full throated cry of a newborn baby signals the beginning of life through its first breath, independently from the navel-base, similarly the loud cry of Jesus indicates the onset of eternal life through the elevation of His consciousness to the highest divine realms.

Moreover, as a newborn child, once it is evolved individually disconnects from the umbilical cord that unites it with its mother and becomes independent, similarly, the Holy Son, being ready to manifest the divinity in Himself separates instantly from His Heavenly Father. Child is carrying the essence of its parents, and during the fascinating progress of evolution, it is utilizing whatever it has been given from them as heritage. It even adds further to it, carrying on the lineage of its family with dignity. Similarly, Jesus carrying the essence of His Father inside Him, is ready to evolve further His lineage and become the glorious chariot of the divine descent on earth. Correspondingly, we are granted, through the teachings of Jesus, to carry His essence and living spirit inside us. Therefore, as His true children we should build our life upon all His commandments and continue His grand lineage. We are the descendants of such precious heritage and it is our prime duty to protect it and even expand it further. How beautifully Jesus has reassured us about the latent divine potential that lies inside us: *John 14:12 "Most certainly I tell you, he who believes in me, the works that I do, he will do also; and he will do greater works than these, because I am going to my Father."*

For each authentic aspirant who craves nothing else than complete liberation, through the manifestation of his divine inherent immortal nature, the current of nectar will follow the same route. Each devotee, by raising his consciousness through steady and one-pointed practice, through unceasing prayer and feverish service to others, gradually will experience the uplifting of his consciousness and ultimately will reach the gate which is the entrance of the abode of the divine. At this stage he will knock at the gate with absolute humility, devotion, renunciation and pure knowledge and he will be well prepared to experience the response to this knock, to tread the threshold of this gate and enter into the vastness of God realization.

The reflection of Jesus' state at a macrocosmic level

The inner state of Jesus Christ is also being reflected at a much more macrocosmic level which is in tune with

His experiences and it participates in the miracle of divine transformation: *Matthew 27:51-52 "Behold, the veil of the temple was torn in two from the top to the bottom. The earth quaked and the rocks were split. The tombs were opened, and many bodies of the saints who had fallen asleep were raised;"* The curtain, that keeps the Holy of The Holies out of sight of everyone, since it is a place preserved solely for God, is torn. This indicates the divine descent on earth, the divinization of the human nature. The earthly body is being replaced by the heavenly body and since this process is not an individual accomplishment rather it happens at a universal level for the sake of whole humankind, there is a grand impact on nature also. The earth shakes and the rocks are split. While Adam and Eve with their distinction from the Creator cause the dominance of grossness and condemn the humankind to mortality, Jesus with His ultimate union with God breaks this dominance.

He actually devastates the root of misery and suffering, which is nothing else than the false identification with the body consciousness and He grants us the nectar of immortality: *Romans 5:17 "For if by the trespass of the one, death reigned through the one; so much more will those who receive the abundance of grace and of the gift of righteousness reign in life through the one, Jesus Christ."* The tombs are also opened indicating that those devotees, who have yearned throughout their past lives for union with God, will merge at the subtle level their consciousness with the divine consciousness. They will experience the inner awakening, under the influence of the vast range of Jesus' inner transformation. Jesus becomes the link which leads to heaven all the souls who have been waiting with longing for union with God, although this inner awakening doesn't reflect at the gross level in their cases. He will accomplish the ultimate victory upon death Himself and also He will have the ability to restore to indestructible life, all those who are related to Him. Not only those who come after Him, but also those who already have died before Him.

The departure of consciousness from the physical body

The death of Christ signifies actually the freedom from the power of sin, from the clutches of ignorance about our true divine nature. Living in fellowship with God, our consciousness expands to higher realms and transforms the grossness of the physical body maintaining the connection between earth and heaven. Normally, our body, full of impurities and bondages due to numerous desires and attachments, is condemned to mortality. At the time of normal death, which may happen due to accidents, physical ailments or gradual decay of the body due to aging, the consciousness – the vital energy – leaves the physical body (which from now on is considered a corpse). It departs through one of the nine orifices in the body. More specifically it comes out from the orifice, which had been more active during the lifetime, on which due to our inclinations we were more focused. For example, the lower orifices of physical body are too active in those who, being deeply engrossed in worldly things, deny the need or even existence of God and perform excessively evil, abominable and corrupted actions, overpowered by animal instincts. Therefore, it is quite possible that one of those orifices will be finally the exit of consciousness at the time of death.

On the other hand, a sincere seeker of the divine truth, who has turned inwards all his senses and is free from all the worldly bindings, will tread consciously the inner path and may stand at the narrow gate. His consciousness can elevate through the upper centers of the body that generally remain close and inactive. However, the ultimate elevation can take place through the divine transformation of the physical body, through resurrection. This deification of the human nature is possible only by the Divine Grace. At this stage, the divine fire penetrates the grossness of the body, burns all the impurities and pierces all the knots that block the way to the narrow gate. The flesh is eaten by this fire while the divine nectar nourishes the transformed immortalized body that reflects through each cell the ultimate victory upon the last enemy, death. A true disciple of Jesus aspires for this ultimate elevation of his consciousness at the uppermost divine realms and for the descent of the divine in his transformed body in this very life. Death becomes just a milestone on the unlimited path of *theosis* and the celestial nectar of the divine descent becomes the fountain of eternal life.

The Divine Nectar

In every sincere servant of the divine will, the fire of immense devotion and craving for God burns all the impurities and opens the way for the flow of His grace. His compassionate reply to this craving comes in the form of His nectar that revives the physical body and liberates it from the clutches of mortality. The divine nectar flowing inside the immortalized body creates a deep sense of intoxication due to the union with God's consciousness. This celestial intoxication overpowers the devotee and takes him in the ocean of divine bliss. The transformed body does not depend any more on any external gross source for its sustenance, since it receives constantly the flow of the divine nectar within it. This nectar nourishes the body, so that it can work as a channel of the divine power on earth. Such an immortalized body becomes a direct link to God for all those who crave to reunite with Him and demolish the ultimate enemy, death: *Revelation 2:11 "He who has an ear, let him hear what the Spirit says to the assemblies. He who overcomes won't be harmed by the second death."*

For a divinized soul the process of death becomes the passage to the eternal life and it is ultimately defeated for once and all. As we have seen in the cases of Christian Saints, being totally aware of the time of their departure from their physical bodies, they welcome in absolute stillness and peace the arrival of the ultimate enemy, death. With burning faith to Jesus, they enter the narrow gate by surrendering everything to their Lord. They are overflowed by the grace of the divine light that descends on them. In a supremely blissful state, uniting with this divine light, they expand their consciousness universally and become lighthouses of inspiration to all those who tread the path of spiritual evolution. Burning all the impurities by the fire of devotional love, they spread the rays of this enormous divine force and empower all the aspirants who can connect with their vibes in a global extent. The divine nectar of their absolute commitment to the Almighty's Will oozes incessantly and keeps alive this force for the ages of the ages and guides all the sincere seekers of the ultimate truth.

The resurrected body of Lord Jesus is the carrier of the divinity and eternally manifests the light of Logos on the physical realm. His human body becomes the most lucid testimony of the divine descent on earth. The human body is rather a temple where God resides. Obviously, His residence— the human body— to hold His immortal and all-pervading nature has to be incorruptible, vast, beyond decomposition and wear. Jesus, becoming the light of the Almighty, spreads through the rays of His complete transformation, the message that the common destiny of all of us is the absolute manifestation of our immortal divine nature, of our latent divine potential beyond any bondage or limitation. The flawless truth of Jesus' message is so perfectly expressed in the *Luke's Gospel 17:20-21*

"Being asked by the Pharisees when the Kingdom of God would come, he answered them, 'The Kingdom of God doesn't come with observation;' neither will they say, 'Look, here!' or, 'Look, there!' for behold, the Kingdom of God is within you.'"

The sin of disobedience to God's command pays its wage which is death, but the union with Jesus Christ and the obedience to His commands offers us the grace of eternal life: *2 Corinthians 5:4-5 "For indeed we who are in this tent do groan, being burdened; not that we desire to be unclothed, but that we desire to be clothed, that what is mortal may be swallowed up by life. Now he who made us for this very thing is God, who also gave to us the down payment of the Spirit."* The grandeur of the resurrection consummates with the most complete and perfect way the essence of Jesus' call to cross the narrow gate and enter into the Kingdom of Heaven that lies within us. All the genuine servants of God have set a perfect example before our eyes and call us with all their love to follow this trail. It is time for us to take the leap and walk on the divine path of resurrection, under their shelter.

THE RESURRECTION OF JESUS CHRIST: HIS ULTIMATE MESSAGE

The climax of divine transformation is presented through the Resurrection of Jesus Christ and it will continue eternally to reveal its grand potential as long there are sincere devotees who believe with innocent childlike faith in the teachings of the divine Shepherd, of Lord Jesus: *John 10:27-28 "My sheep hear my voice, and I know them, and they follow me. I give eternal life to them. They will never perish, and no one will snatch them out of my hand."* Resurrection includes the ultimate message of Jesus Christ and it fulfills all those truths, which have been written in the scriptures and have been stated from Jesus through His teachings. The last enemy, death, is defeated and the heritage of eternal life is granted to all those who yearn to submit their life on the path of immortality.

The Burial of Jesus - The transformation of gross elements

After the crucifixion, when the evening comes Joseph, a disciple of Jesus, asks from Pilate to take the body of his Master in order to bury it, according to the Jewish customs. Joseph takes the body with the help of Nicodemus, wraps it in a new linen sheet and places it in a tomb, which had been recently dug out of solid rock and had never been used before. Then he rolls a large stone across the entrance to the tomb and goes away. Mary Magdalene and Mary, the mother of James, are sitting there, facing the tomb. Everything is set to fulfill the truth of the words that Jesus has foretold when He is asked from some Pharisees to perform a miracle: *Matthew 12:39-40 "But he answered them, "But he answered them, "An evil and adulterous generation seeks after a sign, but no sign will be given it but the sign of Jonah the prophet. For as Jonah was three days and three nights in the belly of the whale, so will the Son of Man be three days and three nights in the heart of the earth."*

Jesus, totally conscious of the divine plan, states that He will spend three days and nights in the depths of earth where the final transfiguration of the gross elements of His physical body will take place. Through this transformation of the physicality, His divine transformation will be completed. This celestial metamorphosis of has a universal impact, which will be also reflected externally at a wider macrocosmic range. It is not an individual achievement, thus it cannot be limited in a person. It is the manifestation of the divine plan for the salvation of the whole humankind.

The entering of Jesus into the depths of earth has an analogy with the case of Jonah. Jonah under God's command is swallowed by a large fish and stays inside its depths, while all the mighty waves roll over him, for three days and nights. He prays unceasingly with all his heart for the glory of God and recognizes that it is only Him that can actually save him. His complete surrender to the divine will brings an end to his permanence inside the fish and God orders the fish to spit Jonah up on the beach. Similarly, Jesus enters into the depths of the earth, while the waves of grossness of the humankind roll over Him. Jesus remains in the earth for three days and nights. During this period, the complete process of divine transformation is fulfilled at three levels, causal, subtle and finally the gross one. As in a complete circle the beginning and the end meet at the same point, yet in a different evolved level, similarly, Jesus starts the process of divine transformation by assuming a physical body, which gradually He divinizes. Ultimately, closing the circle of this divine transformation, He is coming at the first point by reassuming His physical body, which appears to be same, but is completely transfigured. Merging His existence into the divine consciousness, He experiences the gradual transformation of the predominant gross elements of human nature. They are deified and take a subtlest divine form. During the burial of Jesus, the earthly human body which is entangled in mortality gives its place to the heavenly body. The immortalized body reflecting in its each cell the Divine Grace is ultimately saved from the venomous poison of maladies, old age, decay and death.

Buried inside the depths of the earth, Jesus accomplishes the most crucial part of His metamorphosis which is to bring the flesh under the command of the divine will and purify it to such an extent that it will be able to be a chariot of the divine descent. Jesus has submitted His total existence at the feet of His Father and becomes the doorway to all those faithful aspirants who crave for nothing else than union with God. The transformation of the gross elements penetrates all the knots that stand between the human and the super human divine levels. The earth literally is shaken from this process of divine descent receiving the vibrations of Jesus' inner transformation. After the completion of these three days and nights, a powerful earthquake takes place and God brings up to earth Jesus immortalized and divinized even at the physical level.

The next day, after the burial of Jesus, the chief priests and the Pharisees, remembering the words of Jesus: *"The Son of Man is going to be betrayed into human hands, and they will kill him, and on the third day he will be raised"*, meet with Pilate.

They ask from him to order his soldiers to guard Jesus' tomb carefully, until the third day, so that His disciples will not be able to go and steal the body. They believe that Jesus' disciples will do as such and then they will claim publically that their Master has been raised from death. They put a seal on the stone and leave a guard on watch. How amazing is their lack of faith and inability to decipher the truth of Jesus' words and comprehend their vastness! Confined to their individuality, they feel threatened and worried by the blazing flame of Jesus' truths. These truths unravel clearly their hypocrisy towards God and His people. The mind of chief priests and Pharisees is covered from the thick veils of ignorance and arrogance. They believe falsely that they can block the manifestation of the divine plan and prevent the fulfillment of all that has been written from Prophets in the Law of Moses: *Luke 24:46-47 "He said to them, 'Thus it is written, and thus it was necessary for the Christ to suffer and to rise from the dead the third day, and that repentance and remission of sins should be preached in his name to all the nations, beginning at Jerusalem."* Those who yearn to keep their own individuality cannot relate with the grandeur of Jesus' teachings. They even try to muzzle the eternal voice of God which is whispering inside the hearts of all the sincere devotees the ultimate truth: *"You are my child, an inseparable part and parcel of me. I and you are essentially one"*.

Three days after the Burial of Jesus

Very early on Sunday morning, three days after the burial of Jesus, Maria Magdalene and Mary, the mother of James, go to the tomb and find the stone rolled away from the entrance. The body of Jesus Christ is missing from the tomb and the linen clothes are lying empty on the ground: *Luke 24:4-5 "It happened, while they were greatly perplexed about this, behold, two men stood by them in dazzling clothing. Becoming terrified, they bowed their faces down to the earth. They said to them, "Why do you seek the living among the dead?"* How is it possible for the Son of God, who has conquered the uttermost Hades, to live amongst the dead one? How the fountain of eternal life can be confined inside the cave of a tomb? The angel commands the pious women to leave and spread the Good News to Jesus' disciples, saying to them that He has risen from death and He is going to Galilee ahead of them. Both women obey with unquestioning faith to the angel's command and they become the first witnesses of the Resurrection of Jesus: *Matthew 28:9-10 "As they went to tell his disciples, behold, Jesus met them, saying, 'Rejoice!' They came and took hold of his feet, and worshiped him. Then Jesus said to them, 'Don't be afraid. Go tell my brothers that they should go into Galilee, and there they will see me.'"* The inner purity and sincerity of their hearts enables these loyal women to face the glory of the immortal and resurrected body of Jesus. Because of the purity of their heart and unquestioning faith to their Master, they deserve to see the ultimate truth incarnated in the immortalized Christ.

On that same day, Jesus appears before two of His followers also who are going to a village named Emmaus very close to Jerusalem. Initially, they cannot recognize it is Jesus and they talk with Him as a common man. Unaware that their Master is standing before their eyes, they inform Him about all that has taken place during the last days at Jerusalem. They even share with Him their grief for the death of their Master and their amazement about the news that Jesus has been raised from death. They ask Jesus to stay with them still not knowing who He is. On the way to their home, Jesus explains to them the truths of the Holy Scriptures. Eventually, during their meal they become able to recognize Him: *Luke 24:30-32 "It happened, that when he had sat down at the table with them, he took the bread and gave thanks. Breaking it, he gave to them. Their eyes were opened, and they recognized him, and he vanished out of their sight. They said one to another, 'Weren't our hearts burning within us, while he spoke to us along the way, and while he opened the Scriptures to us?'"* Both disciples realize that the one who has offered them this burning storm of inspiration while explaining the scriptures is no one else than their Master. The moment they realize who He is that very moment Jesus is gone from their sight. Jesus blesses with the glory of His resurrected body all His children who have pure faith in Him, so that the fire of their devotion and faith will be invigorated further and aspire them to walk with more zeal on the path of ultimate truth.

Resurrected Jesus appears before His disciples

After the vision of His resurrected form, the two followers get up at once and go back to Jerusalem where they find the eleven disciples being gathered together at one place. They inform them that their Master has defeated the ultimate enemy, death, and He has been resurrected: *Luke 24:36-39 "As they said these things, Jesus himself stood among them, and said to them, 'Peace be to you.' But they were terrified and filled with fear, and supposed that they had seen a spirit. He said to them, "Why are you troubled? Why do doubts arise in your hearts? See my hands and my feet, that it is truly me. Touch me and see, for a spirit doesn't have flesh and bones, as you see that I have."'* Jesus understands their wonder, fear and doubt and to make them certain that He is not a ghost rather He carries a resurrected physical form, He asks them to touch Him and He shows to them His hands and feet. To dispel the doubts in their hearts and minds He asks them to approach Him and feel His tangible presence at physical level by touching Him.

As incense, after being burnt, may keep its initial shape, still it has lost its grossness completely, similarly the immortalized body of Jesus maintains its past form, yet it is totally renewed. It is free from any external dependence, disease, corruption, old age and death. It is full of divine light and celestial beauty, dispelling the gloomy grossness and removing all the limits imposed by it. It can still perform all the external activities, yet it is completely free and independent from them now even for the sake of its sustenance and survival. For an immortalized body even the most trivial activity is a precious part of the grand and unlimited divine plan and its only purpose is the evolution of his consciousness. Free from any external dependence, it is sustained through the divine nectar that oozes unceasingly inside Him, due to the constant holy communion with God. However, such an immortalized body, facing no limitation, bondage or restriction, can consume even solid food. Still, there is no accumulation of waste in it. As everything put inside the blazing fire turns to fire, due to its fierce flames, similarly, the penetrating fire, which is awakened inside the divinized body of Jesus, swallows everything and transforms it to divine nectar. Therefore, to strengthen their faith and make them certain that He is not a spirit but a physically resurrected body, Jesus asks to eat with them. A spirit, carrying a subtle form, would obviously not be able to consume gross nourishment. This is why Jesus asks them to eat with them, to remove any doubt from their heart and mind: *Luke 24:40-43 "When he had said this, he showed them his hands and his feet. While they still didn't believe for joy, and wondered, he said to them, 'Do you have anything here to eat?' They gave him a piece of a broiled fish and some honeycomb. He took them, and ate in front of them."* Filled with innermost joy for the reappearance of their beloved Master, they receive the Holy Spirit from the One who has the complete authority in heaven and on earth:

Mark 16:15-16 "He said to them, "Go into all the world, and preach the Good News to the whole creation. He who believes and is baptized will be saved; but he who disbelieves will be condemned."

Reappearance of Resurrected Jesus before Thomas and other disciples

One of His disciples, Thomas, is not present at the first appearance of Jesus before the disciples. Therefore, he claims that unless he sees the scars of the nails in His hands and puts his finger on those scars and his hand in His side he will not believe that His master has really resurrected: *John 20:26-29 "After eight days again his disciples were inside, and Thomas was with them. Jesus came, the doors being locked, and stood in the midst, and said, 'Peace be to you.' Then he said to Thomas, 'Reach here your finger, and see my hands. Reach here your hand, and put it into my side. Don't be unbelieving, but believing.' Thomas answered him, 'My Lord and my God!' Jesus said to him, 'Because you have seen me, you have believed. Blessed are those who have not seen, and have believed.'"* Jesus appears before the eyes of Thomas with a miraculous way that is indicative of His divinized state. Despite of His tangible physical form, there is no grossness in His body. The grossness of His physicality has been burnt by the fire of the divine union and is transformed to the subtlest form. Therefore, there is no physical limitation for Him and He can pass through the door although it is closed.

At this juncture, it is noticeable that in this dialogue of Jesus with Thomas it is not mentioned that Jesus still has the scars of the nails in His hands. How could this be possible? How could His totally transformed body carry any past sign of decay, corruption and wear? All such past signs has been extinguished from the blazing divine fire that has penetrated each iota of His gross body. Further, just to convince Thomas about His physical presence, Jesus asks him to touch His hands and side. A spirit would not be tangible as He is. Thomas overwhelmed by the radiation of His Master's immortalized form, surrenders by seeing the glory of His celestial state. Now he believes with all his heart that before him stands Lord Jesus. However, Jesus so beautifully explains to him that the fountain of real faith lies in the purity of heart and not in the visible proofs and signs.

Through His divine transformation, Jesus becomes the channel through which all the devotees can have a direct link to the primordial source, to His Heavenly Father. God has descended on Him and whoever believes and understands Him can be united with the divine. His immortalized body, after the resurrection, has been totally transubstantiated and does not carry any physical substance. All the bondages of His past earthly body have been demolished: *1 Corinthians 15:47 "The first man is of the earth, made of dust. The second man is the Lord from heaven."* This ultimate metamorphosis from a physical to a heavenly body has swallowed within it the darkness of mortality. Now the light of divinity has spread its rays to every part of this magnificent creation!

Last appearance of Resurrected Jesus before His disciples

Before He is taken up to heaven, Jesus appears one more time in front of His disciples at the lake Tiberias. There Simon Peter, Thomas, Nathanael, the sons of Zebedee, and two other disciples of Jesus have gone fishing and they spend the whole night in the boat without catching a thing. Jesus appears before them and asks them to throw their net on the right side of the boat so that they can catch some fishes. When they recognize that it is their Master who is talking to them they approach with joy and Jesus asks them to come and eat. This is the third time that Jesus appears before them after being raised from death. Jesus, being certain of the burning devotional love of Peter, asks from him to take care of His sheep. From now on, the Apostles will become themselves the shepherds who will open the narrow gate to all those faithful and sincere aspirants who seek the ultimate truth; to those deserving candidates who wish to become a carrier of the divine descent, as their Master did, and who longingly crave to tread the immortal path. Jesus asks them to remain all together in Jerusalem. The time is ripe now to experience the descent of the Holy Spirit upon them, which will enable them to convey His teachings to the masses, to exhibit, out of compassion, all His supernatural powers and even more. This forthcoming experience will pour in their hearts the feverish strength to spread to all the nations the Good News of divine transformation and resurrection: *Luke 24:49 "Behold, I send forth the promise of my Father on you. But wait in the city of Jerusalem until you are clothed with power from on high."*

The immortal mission which has been established by Jesus has such an expansive range that is eternally working in every era through the divine servants who have sacrificed their personal will. It is flowing through all those who have surrendered their heart, mind, soul and might to the God's command. Jesus leads His disciples out of the city as far as Bethany, blesses them with His hands, fills them with supreme joy and inner power and departs from them being taken up to heaven, being merged in totality into the divine's ocean. Jesus grants them the life-giving water that oozes eternally and blesses them with His divine energy so they can inspire all those who are ready to dive into the core of His teaching: *Acts 13:35 "[…]'You will not allow your faithful servant to see decay."*

The Descent of Holy Spirit

Fifty days after His Resurrection, the disciples experience the descent of the Holy Spirit, as their Master has foretold, and the divine power is poured into them: *Acts 2:1-4 "Now when the day of Pentecost had come, they were all with one accord in one place. Suddenly there came from the sky a sound like the rushing of a mighty wind, and it filled all the house where they were sitting. Tongues like fire appeared and were distributed to them, and one sat on each of them. They were all filled with the Holy Spirit, and began to speak with other languages, as the Spirit gave them the ability to speak."* From now on the servants of Jesus live in fellowship with Him and they have an eternal contact with His energy. They live, exist and evolve inside and through Him. All their actions are performed under the light of the ultimate goal of Jesus' mission. They serve humankind for its divine evolution, aspiring them to unravel its divine potential. The tongues of devotional fire above their heads inspire them to be courageous enough to face all the adversities on the path of immortality. This fire transforms the grossness of their existence, thus, their divine transformation begins so that they can go beyond the clutches of death and decay. Jesus grants to them the life-giving ambrosia which emanates from within and sustains them eternally.

It is important to note at this point how the divine appearance transforms the elements in nature and is being reflected through them at a very subtle level. The elements vibrate with the light of the primordial source, Logos, and become direct channels, which reflect the manifestation of the divine on earth. Initially, there is the sound which actually spreads the message of the divine descent, it is the Logos, the Word. The element of ether transmits the current of the ultimate energy which sustains everything and through the sound, a link between the subtle form and the gross form of energy is being established. Then the element of air signifies the process of God's descent. The wind spreads to all the directions, actually purifies and sanctifies all the impurities, penetrates the soul. With its blowing, it is taking away all the obstructions that could block the way to God-realization. Subsequently, the element of fire, through the form of blazing tongues of Divine Grace, spreads the light of pure knowledge and discrimination to the sincere disciples of God. It burns all the impurities and eradicates all the roots of the subtle filths that are burnt from its passage and its intense flame.

Accordingly, the fire penetrates the elements of water and earth which are actually predominant in the physical world, thus, their transformation is extremely crucial and difficult for the path of mission immortality. The fire actually consumes the grossness of water and earth and purifies them through this transformation of their physicality. Owing to this fire, many supernatural abilities are witnessed in those who tread the path of immortality. They are not affected even if they consume poison, since they are able to transform it to nectar, they can levitate in air or float in water since this fire of God realization has eaten the grossness of the physical body. It is again this fire which empowers the devotees to be totally disconnected from outer sources of nourishment or other external means. They can survive by imbibing the divine nectar in order to serve the humankind and guide those who seek to attain God-realization. Fire melts the nectar which emanates from the higher centers within us and it propels the flowing of this nectar throughout the whole body till the lowest parts. With this way, the total existence of a sincere devotee will become a temple of God and it will exhibit its absolute freedom, its fusion with Him through each single cell. The five elements-ether, air, fire, water, earth- reflect, through their deepest transformation, the divine's descent and glorify the fulfillment of Jesus' ultimate message on earth.

The Divine devotional fire

Initially, through the path of selfless service the devotees, who consciously submit their life into Christ hands, set the ground for the manifestation of the divine fire. Melting the ego and their personal will into the feverish heat of unceasing altruistic service, such true devotees offer gradually the required fuel for the revelation of the inner divine flames. Through austerities, celibacy and continence they accomplish the freedom from the clutches of sensual pleasures. Temperance and service prepare the fertile soil for the inflorescence of relentless prayer. The mental purification and the cultivation of compassion towards all, constitute the prolific soil for the blooming of the seed of unceasing chanting of the God's name and the awakening of the innermost devotional fire.

The constant longing for the divine and the continuous current of invocation of His grace, which flows inside the hearts of the sincere aspirants, transfer the verbal chanting of God's name to deeper subtle levels *Psalms 84:1-2 "How lovely are your dwellings, Lord of hosts! My soul longs, and even faints for the courts of the Lord. My heart and my flesh cry out for the living God."* The talk to God crosses the means of external expressions and the actual chanting is happening with each breath which glorifies the divine's grandeur. The yearning for our reunion with our Father lights the fire of surrendering to God's will and qualifies the practitioner to become an authentic instrument in the hands of God. The flesh of individuality and ego is being eaten from this fire of absolute surrender.

The fire of devotion and worship swallows within it all the impurities, sanctifies the grossness and refines the totality of the aspirant. He doesn't exist anymore as a separate individuality since, literally, each cell of his body is an instrument for the fulfillment of the divine plan. The fire of dedication and pure love for the divine melts all the spiritual obstacles, all the downwards tendencies and passions and leads to the actual purification at a physical level. The body of Jesus becomes the bread of eternal life and the nectar of God realization intoxicates the devotee with the blissful wine of devoted loyalty and commitment to God's command: *Psalms 36:7-9 "How precious is your loving kindness, God! The children of men take refuge under the shadow of your wings. They shall be abundantly satisfied with the abundance of your house. You will make them drink of the river of your pleasures. For with you is the spring of life. In your light shall we see light."*

The infinite range of mission immortality

The mission immortality established from Jesus Christ expands to such an extent that it embraces each being in the whole universe. The Second Coming of Jesus is a reality for all those who sincerely wish to tread the path of divine descent at every level, even the physical one. Everyone is included and affected by the presence of these divine shepherds, whose guiding compassion is endless, limitless and inexhaustible.

The immortal path meets no bondage, no limitation. It lies beyond any dogmatic approach and spreads through all the levels, let that be physical, mental, intellectual or spiritual. The ultimate message of Jesus for divine transformation and descent of God in each iota of our existence is as bright, as vast, as expansive are the rays of divine light. In every era, the compassionate Almighty will grant us with His precious servants, whose example can permeate within us a storm of burning faith, steadfast determination and supreme love for each other.

Glory and honor to all those who have served, serve, will serve this mission! May we tread this immortal path and experience the grandeur of resurrection and divine transformation, under the guidance and the shelter of competent Masters, of authentic servants of Lord. Amen!

Psalms 103:22

"Praise the Lord, all his creatures,
in all places of his dominion.
Praise the Lord, my soul!"

EPILOGUE

Dear reader,

Dear brother and sister,

The pages of this book may have reached to the end, but the path of *theosis,* of the divine descent on earth, under the compassionate guidance of Jesus, meets no end, no limitation.

From tender age I used to wonder how we can set limits for God who has created everything and yet stays aloof from all this. Believing that the sense of impossibility is just the beginning of infinite possibilities, I got deeply inspired by the motto used by the revolutionary students in Paris in 1968: *"Let's be realistic! Let's fulfill the impossible!",* an inspiration that stuck in my heart and since then it has become the compass in life.

Growing up in Greece, in an orthodox Christian family, I always carried deep love and appreciation for Jesus and His teachings. Still, it was until I met my spiritual elder, Swami Buddh Puri Ji Maharaj, that the seed of unconditional faith in Jesus actually sprouted inside me.

Studying the Holy Bible with him, the grandeur of Jesus' call – for the resurrection, the divine descent at every level of our existence, even the gross one – has been realized. Living close to Maharaj Ji, I have often witnessed physical evidences of this gradual transformation in his body – spending long periods in solitude without any external provision and free from hunger, thirst, sleep and effect of heat or cold. Furthermore, his body has never shown any sign of disease or aging in terms of physical strength and energy despite running in late 60s. Moreover, experiencing in myself how the devotional prayer and practice can cure even our gross diseases, I feel intensively aspired by the vastness of the latent divine potential that lies inside each one of us. For example, serving education for more than 12 years, it was truly admirable to listen often the young students wondering from the fact that during the whole year they had not seen me even once falling sick, being full of energy and wellness. These all have fueled my aspiration to walk the path of immortality that Jesus has paved for all of us. Additionally, they have motivated me to continue further the research upon the practices of the Christian Saints and present it, by the Divine Grace, in a new volume.

Dear readers, the divine wind is blowing. Let's not delay anymore the journey to eternal life, under the light of Jesus' teachings. Let's be realistic, let's fulfill the impossible! Amen!

One of His children
Despoina Tsaousi

Printed in the United States
By Bookmasters